D0482203

This book is due on the last date stamped below.
Failure to return books on the date due may
result in assessment of overdue fees.

MAY 2 4 1999

JUN 0 7 REC'D

FINES .50 per day

ALSO BY GERTRUDE HIMMELFARB

Poverty and Compassion: The Moral Imagination of the Late Victorians (1991)
The New History and the Old (1987)
Marriage and Morals Among the Victorians (1986)
The Idea of Poverty: England in the Early Industrial Age (1984)
On Liberty and Liberalism: The Case of John Stuart Mill (1974)
Victorian Minds (1968)
Darwin and the Darwinian Revolution (1959)
Lord Acton: A Study in Conscience and Politics (1952)

EDITOR OF

John Stuart Mill, *On Liberty* (1974)
John Stuart Mill, *Essays on Politics and Culture* (1962)
T. R. Malthus, *On Population* (1960)
Lord Acton, *Essays on Freedom and Power* (1948)

ON
LOOKING
INTO
THE ABYSS

ON
LOOKING
INTO
THE ABYSS

Untimely Thoughts on
Culture and Society

GERTRUDE
HIMMELFARB

Alfred A. Knopf   New York   1994

Essays in this volume were originally published in the
following:
The American Scholar: "On Looking into the Abyss" (as
"The Abyss Revisited") and "Liberty: 'One Very Simple
Principle'?"
Commentary: "Of Heroes, Villains, and Valets."
The National Interest: "The Dark and Bloody Crossroads
Where Nationalism and Religion Meet."
The New York Times Book Review: "Where Have All the
Footnotes Gone?"
The Times Literary Supplement: "Postmodernist History" (as
"Telling It As You Like It").

Library of Congress Cataloging-in-Publication Data
Himmelfarb, Gertrude.
On looking into the Abyss: untimely thoughts on
culture and society / by Gertrude Himmelfarb.—1st ed.
p. cm.
ISBN 0-679-42826-7
1. United States—Intellectual life—20th century.
2. United States—Civilization—1970–   I. Title.
E162.12.H56 1994
973.9—dc20   93-4928
                                    CIP

Manufactured in the United States of America
Published February 7, 1994
Reprinted Once
Third Printing, March 1994

To the Memory of
Lionel Trilling

Contents

Introduction

Only after completing this book did I realize how prominently Lionel Trilling figures in it. The title of the book (derived from the lead essay) is a direct quotation from him. The title of another of the essays is an adaptation from him. And most of the other essays cite him at crucial points of the argument. In dedicating this book to him, I am discharging an intellectual and personal debt that is long overdue.

I was never a student of Trilling's, but I was an admirer and a friend. (It was one of his many virtues that his friendships knew no limits of age.) In recent years I find myself returning to his writings more and more, not so much for inspiration as for solace. The inspiration came many years ago when I learned to appreciate a mode of thought that I now recognize—I did not know this at the time—to be uniquely his: a seriousness about ideas that was not "academic" (defying both the language of academia and the compartmentalization of disciplines); a seriousness about public affairs that went beyond (or stopped short of) politics in the ordinary sense; a moral *gravitas* that was surely unseemly when I was younger but that may be more appropriate at my present age (and in the present time).

If I now find solace in Trilling, it is because he was able to resist the insidious ideological and political fashions of his time without the coarsening of mind that often comes with doing battle, and also without the timidity and equivocation that retreats from battle in an excess of fastidiousness. What I have come to realize more recently is that he was not only remarkably clearheaded about the threats to intellectual integrity and political liberty in his day; he was also remarkably prescient in recognizing the first signs of the new perils that have replaced the old.

In an earlier book, *Poverty and Compassion*, I adopted Trilling's much quoted phrase "the moral imagination" for the subtitle, and the passage in which that expression appears for the book's epigraph. Rereading that passage today, I am impressed once again by its wisdom. Nearly half a century ago, when the welfare state was young and "democratic socialism" was not yet the oxymoron it has become, Trilling foresaw the fallacy in what then seemed to be an enlightened, humane, and compassionate social policy. Almost in passing, in the course of discussing quite another subject, he made an observation that is of the greatest pertinence today:

> Some paradox of our natures leads us, when once we have made our fellow men the objects of our enlightened interest, to go on to make them the objects of our pity, then of our wisdom, ultimately of our coercion. It is to prevent this corruption, the most ironic and tragic that man knows, that we stand in need of the moral realism which is the product of the free play of the moral imagination.[1]

In the present book, I have had occasion again and again to draw upon the sense of "moral realism" that is so much a part of Trilling's "moral imagination": in the lead essay, where his image of the abyss invites us to reflect on the intellectual arrogance and spiritual impoverishment of some of the latest tendencies in literary criticism, philosophy, and history; in the essay on heroes, in which he is quoted as exposing the fatal weakness of structuralism long before it had even acquired that name; in the essay on nationalism, where the literary critic lectures the historian on the fallacies of the "long view," in which murder and torture seem not so terrible as they compose themselves into a "meaningful pattern."[2] Only by an oversight do the essays on Mill (his "one very simple principle" of liberty) and on Marx (his "standing Hegel on his head") fail to invoke Trilling, who repeatedly warned against the simplification, abstraction, and impoverishment of both liberalism and Marxism.[3]

If Lionel Trilling's presence is so conspicuous in this book, so is the memory of the Holocaust. This too was not anticipated or consciously intended by me. Yet it now seems to me perfectly natural and proper. In almost every essay, the Holocaust stands as a rebuke to historians, philosophers, and literary critics who, in their zeal for one or another of the intellectual fashions of our time, belittle or demean one of the greatest tragedies of all time. Historians who think it the highest calling of their profession to resurrect the "daily life of ordinary people" can find little evidence in the daily life of ordinary Germans of the overwhelming fact of life—and of death—for millions of Jews; those who look for the "long-term" processes and impersonal "structures" in history tend to explain this "short-term event" in such a way as to explain it away; and those seeking to "deconstruct" the history of the Holocaust as they deconstruct all of history come perilously close to the "revisionists" who deny the reality of the Holocaust.

And so with philosophers and literary critics for whom there is no reality but only language, no philosophy but only a play of mind, no morality but only rhetoric and aesthetics. It is said of one of the most eminent of these philosophers-cum-critics, Paul de Man, that he "looked into the abyss and came away smiling"—which might have prepared us for the revelation that during the war he had been a Nazi collaborator and anti-Semite, but not, perhaps, for the tortuous apologetics of some of his disciples. An even more eminent elder of this school (and an even more outspoken and unrepentant Nazi), Martin Heidegger, said that the abyss is to be found in the sentence "Language speaks," and that in that abyss man can make his "dwelling place" and be "at home." One of Heidegger's admirers, Richard Rorty, is repelled by his Nazism and finds him personally a "nasty piece of work," but does not permit these disagreeable facts to detract from his philosophy. Instead Rorty deduces from him such lessons as that philosophy must not be "taken seriously," that the traditional subjects of philosophy (morality as well as metaphysics) should be approached "playfully," "light-mindedly," and that only a "metaphysical prig" believes in such things as "truth" and "reality."[4]

Perhaps this book should be labeled "The Confessions of an Unregenerate Prig," for it is dedicated to the proposition that there are such things as truth and reality and that there is a connection between them, as there is also a connection between the aesthetic sensibility and the moral imagination, between culture and society. We all pay lip service to the adage "Ideas have consequences," but it is only in extremis that we take it seriously, when the ideas of Stalin or Hitler issue in the realities of gulags and death camps. It is the premise of this book that well short of such dire situations there is an intimate, pervasive relationship between what happens in our schools and universities, in the intellectual and artistic communities, and what happens in society and the polity.

The essays in this volume, in their original form, were all written and either published or delivered as lectures within a three-year period. This may account for the fact that although they deal with different subjects—history, philosophy, and literature; liberalism, Marxism, nationalism, and postmodernism—they circle around some of the same ideas.

A common criticism of discussions of cultural issues such as these is that they are too often anecdotal or trivial, focusing on unimportant episodes and unrepresentative views. I have tried to avoid this by addressing, seriously and respectfully (if also sometimes critically), the work of the most eminent and gifted scholars, as influential outside the academy as within.

I have taken the liberty of extensively revising and expanding the essays; some are half again as long as their original versions. This reflects not only my own obsessive habits of rewriting and revising but also the subjects themselves. Neither the original essay on the abyss nor that on postmodernist history, for example, had any mention of the "deconstruction" of the Holocaust, for the simple reason that that intellectual enterprise emerged only after the initial composition of those essays.

One lesson that was confirmed for me while preparing this volume is how rapidly academic disciplines change and intellectual fashions evolve. I first learned that lesson soon after the publication of my book *The New History and the Old*, in 1987. In a lecture the following year I ventured to suggest (what I had not said explicitly in the book) that the next stage in the evolution of the "new history" would be the "deconstruction" of history. My audience, which included some distinguished historians, ridiculed that idea. Surely no real historian, I was told (this was meant to exclude a well-known philosopher of history who, it was agreed, did not qualify as a historian), could possibly do anything so absurd. Within a year, more and more historians, and not only philosophers of history, were doing just that. (Some had been doing that earlier, but no one noticed.) Even I, prepared for that development, was not prepared, either emotionally or intellectually, for the next logical step, the deconstruction of the Holocaust. Now I can only wonder where the next "cutting edge" of the discipline will be, what the "moving finger" will write and, having writ, move on—to express what new audacity, to usher in what post-postmodernity?

Each of these essays recalls the special circumstances that produced it and the individuals who inspired it. If the spirit of Lionel Trilling hovers over the book as a whole, it is most visible in the title essay, "On Looking into the Abyss."[5] When I first read the essay by Trilling in which that image appeared, I took it, as he ostensibly presented it, as a commentary on the teaching of modern literature.[6] Thirty years later I take it as I now think he intended it: as a commentary on the culture in general, and not only on the culture but on the society that reflects that culture.

"Of Heroes, Villains, and Valets" was delivered in May 1991 as the Jefferson Lecture sponsored by the National Endowment for the Humanities.[7] (The first in that series, as it happened, was delivered by Lionel Trilling almost twenty years earlier.) I am indebted to the council of the Endowment, which selected me for that great honor, and to the chairman, Lynne Cheney, who, during her tenure of office, courageously promoted a view of the humanities that she, like Trilling, derived from their common hero, Matthew Arnold.

"From Marx to Hegel" was delivered at the American Enterprise Institute in May 1990 in the Bradley Lectureship series.[8] In that lecture I commented on the surprising appearance of Hegel on the Washington scene. I might also have remarked on the intellectual vitality generated by the Bradley Lectures in a city not notable for intellectual pursuits.

"Liberty: 'One Very Simple Principle'?" was written for a colloquium organized by the Institut für die Wissenschaften vom Menschen to have been held at Castel Gandolfo in

August 1992.[9] It was a heady thought—to speak on that subject in the presence of Pope John Paul II and to hear the pope's comments. Unfortunately, the pope was taken ill and the colloquium met instead in Vienna. Although I was not present, my paper was distributed and has been published in the volume of essays prepared for that occasion.

"The Dark and Bloody Crossroads Where Nationalism and Religion Meet" was presented at a conference of the National Review Institute at Fiesole in October 1992, memorably presided over by Margaret Thatcher.[10] The title was suggested by a comment by Lionel Trilling (in the unlikely context of a discussion of Theodore Dreiser and Henry James) on "the dark and bloody crossroads where literature and politics meet."[11] The conference was appropriately held (given my theme) in a former monastery, which provided a beautiful and tranquil background for a most troublesome subject.

"Where Have All the Footnotes Gone?" started as a jeu d'esprit and became something more than that, both in the writing of it and in its reception.[12] Published in June 1991, it produced more letters than anything else I have written—and letters written with greater passion than one would think such a subject would inspire. A great number of people apparently cherish fond memories of Kate Turabian, the supreme arbiter of footnoting, and recall with nostalgia her severe but loving (as it now seems to them) regime. If there was any criticism of my piece, it was because I had neglected to mention some particular rule deemed essential to what one correspondent called "a beautifully crafted footnote."

"Postmodernist History" originated as a paper for a conference on "Tradition and Creativity in Contemporary Culture" held by the Institute on Religion and Public Life in May 1992.[13] I am grateful to Father Richard Neuhaus for provoking me to write at length on a subject I had only skirted about before, and for obliging me to read a good deal of literature that was neither readable nor congenial but that proved to be very instructive.

I am grateful to all those who provided the occasions for the writing and publication of these essays. My research assistant, Elizabeth Anderson, was of invaluable assistance in tracking down elusive books, photocopying articles, checking references, and even instructing me in the finer points of word-processing; it has been a delight to work with someone so intelligent and conscientious, a rare combination of virtues. I am also indebted to my editor, Ashbel Green, for his good counsel and judgment, in connection not only with this book but with all my others he has seen through the press in the past twenty-five years. There cannot be many editor-author relationships that have been so consistently and thoroughly agreeable over so long a period of time. Nor are there many other publishing firms that maintain such high standards of editing; Miss Turabian would have been proud of my copy-editor, Melvin Rosenthal.

Finally, once again, I must express my immeasurable debt to my husband, Irving Kristol. It seems eminently fitting to me that we should have celebrated our fiftieth wedding anniversary (I cannot quite believe this but I am assured it is so) just as I started to prepare this volume. It is also fitting that our fourth grandchild should have been born just as I put the finishing touches to it. It is not, however, fitting to dedicate a book entitled *On Looking into the Abyss* to a beloved husband and family. Perhaps I can repair this omission in my next book, on the more suitable subject of "Victorian virtues."

ON
LOOKING
INTO
THE ABYSS

I

On Looking into the Abyss

IN A NOW classic essay, "On the Teaching of Modern Literature," Lionel Trilling described his students' response to his own course on modern literature:

> I asked them to look into the Abyss, and, both dutifully and gladly, they have looked into the Abyss, and the Abyss has greeted them with the grave courtesy of all objects of serious study, saying: "Interesting, am I not? And *exciting*, if you consider how deep I am and what dread beasts lie at my bottom. Have it well in mind that a knowledge of me contributes materially to your being whole, or well-rounded, men."[1]

The subjects of that course were the modernist greats: Yeats, Eliot, Joyce, Proust, Kafka, Lawrence, Mann, Gide,

Conrad. By way of background, Trilling had his students also read some of the seminal works that prepared the way for the modernists: Frazer's *Golden Bough*, Nietzsche's *Birth of Tragedy* and *Genealogy of Morals*, Freud's *Civilization and Its Discontents*, Diderot's *Rameau's Nephew*, Dostoyevsky's *Notes from Underground*, Tolstoy's *Death of Ivan Ilyitch*. Each of these, the literary and philosophical works alike, was profoundly subversive of culture, society, morality, conventional sexuality—of all that which was once confidently called "civilization." These were the "dread beasts" lurking at the bottom of the "Abyss." And it was this abyss that the students "dutifully and gladly"—and intelligently—looked into and found "interesting," even "exciting."

Trilling's point was that such a course, the teaching of such books, was self-defeating, for it transformed what should have been a profound spiritual and emotional experience into an academic exercise. Instead of hearing the writer's "wild cry" of terror, passion, mystery, rage, rapture, despair, the students heard themselves (and perhaps their professor) discoursing, seriously and sophisticatedly, about *Angst*, alienation, authenticity, sensibility. The result was to vitiate the works themselves and bring about precisely the opposite of their intended effect: "the socialization of the anti-social, or the acculturation of the anti-cultural, or the legitimization of the subversive."[2]

The image of the abyss haunted the most subversive author on Trilling's reading list, Nietzsche, and Nietzsche's most subversive hero, Zarathustra.

Man is a rope stretched between the animal and the Superman—a rope over an abyss.

Courage slayeth also giddiness at abysses: and where doth man not stand at abysses! Is not seeing itself—seeing abysses?

Ye are frightened: do your hearts turn giddy? Doth the
abyss here yawn for you? Doth the hell-hound here yelp
at you?

He who seeth the abyss, but with eagle's eyes—he who
with eagle's talons *graspeth* the abyss: he hath courage.[3]

The same image is at the heart of *The Birth of Tragedy*, an
account of the primal, tragic, "unnatural crime" epitomized
by the myth of Oedipus and revealed by the "wisdom" of
Dionysus. Because that crime is so monstrous, the wisdom
that recognizes and embraces it is equally criminal, for "who-
ever, in pride of knowledge, hurls nature into the abyss of
destruction, must himself experience nature's disintegra-
tion." Those who do not have the courage of a Dionysus,
who lack the "divine frenzy" of the artist or poet, may take
refuge in the serene philosophy of Apollo or in Sophocles'
version of the myth, which superimposes upon it "the lumi-
nous afterimage which kind nature provides our eyes after
a look into the abyss." Nietzsche, however, looking into that
abyss with the open eyes of Dionysus, sees it as pure tragedy.

Indeed, my friends, believe with me in this Dionysiac
life and in the rebirth of tragedy! Socratic man has run
his course; crown your heads with ivy, seize the thyrsus,
and do not be surprised if tiger and panther lie down
and caress your feet! Dare to lead the life of tragic
man, and you will be redeemed.[4]

This is what Trilling's students were reading and what
they glibly translated into the fashionable vocabulary of the
time, thus domesticating the wild beasts and inuring themselves to the terrors of the abyss. This approach to the abyss,
Trilling observed on another occasion, reminded him of a
practical, responsible householder: "Having come to take

nullity for granted, he wants to be enlightened and entertained by statements about the nature of nothing, what its size is, how it is furnished, what services the management provides, what sort of conversation and amusements can go on in it."[5] Nietzsche himself anticipated just this response when he mocked the aesthetes who engaged in "so much loose talk about art and [had] so little respect for it," who used "Beethoven and Shakespeare as subjects for light conversation."[6]

Nietzsche wrote more than a century ago; Trilling a few decades ago. Since then the abyss has grown deeper and more perilous, with new and more dreadful terrors lurking at the bottom. The beasts of modernism have mutated into the beasts of postmodernism—relativism into nihilism, amorality into immorality, irrationality into insanity, sexual deviancy into polymorphous perversity. And since then, generations of intelligent students under the guidance of their enlightened professors have looked into the abyss, have contemplated those beasts, and have said, "How interesting, how exciting."

Rereading Trilling's essay, I was struck by how pertinent it is to the present state of the academic culture; indeed, it is more pertinent now than it was in his own day. Trilling was troubled by the ease with which great books were emasculated (a word one hardly dares use today), the way passionate affirmations were reduced to rote formulas and subversive ideas made banal and respectable. But his students were at least reading those books and confronting those ideas. One cannot say that now with any confidence.

Today, students in some of the most distinguished departments of literature are all too often reading books about how to read books. Literary theory has replaced literature itself as the fashionable subject of study. Structuralism and deconstruction, gender theory and the new historicism, reader-response and speech-act theory—these are more hotly debated than the content and style of particular novels or poems. And when novels or poems are the ostensible subject of discussion, the theorists are so dominant ("hegemonic" or "privileged," as they would say), so insistent upon their superiority over author and work alike, that their comments on the latter are little more than commentaries on their own modes of criticism.

A book by one prominent theorist, Jonathan Culler, opens with a chapter entitled "Beyond Interpretation," suggesting that the interpretation of individual works is beneath the consideration of the serious theorist, is indeed an impediment to theory. "Formerly," Culler observes elsewhere, "the history of criticism was part of the history of literature . . . now the history of literature is part of the history of criticism."[7] Another eminent professor, Gerald Graff, reasons that since the various literary theories are irreconcilable, the only solution is to make them the focus of instruction, and this in undergraduate as well as graduate classes.[8] Lionel Trilling would have felt confirmed in his worst fears by this proposal, which elevates theory not only above the literary work but even above any interpretation of that work. He would also have savored the irony of the title of Graff's influential book *Professing Literature*—not reading or appreciating or understanding literature, but "professing" it; or, more ironic still, the former president of the Modern Language Association, Barbara Herrnstein Smith, who refers to the years in which she "professed" Shakespeare's sonnets.[9] (Trilling's own anthology of great literature is fittingly entitled *The Experience of Literature*.)

Moreover, the literature that is "professed," when theorists condescend to discuss actual works of literature, are "texts"—the very word denigrating both the idea of literature and the idea of greatness. As a text, Superman is as worthy of study as Shakespeare, or an obscure woman writer (obscure for good literary reasons) as meritorious as George Eliot (who is suspect not only because she assumed that male pseudonym but because she made a profession of being a writer rather than a feminist-writer). A graduate student at Louisiana State University, mindful of the grand tradition in that university epitomized by Cleanth Brooks, Robert Penn Warren, and *The Southern Review*, was dismayed to discover that their successors, determined to open the "canon" to women and black writers, have little concern with the literary merit of their books and no passion or even enthusiasm for the books themselves. They are, she finds, more interested in making political statements than literary ones, and more interested in theory than in literature—any kind of literature. Given the assignment to "deconstruct something," one enterprising student chose to deconstruct the game "Trivial Pursuit," to the professor's delight.[10]

If literature is what theorists choose to call it, it is not surprising that interpretation (when they deign to interpret) is what they make of it. One of the gurus of this school, Stanley Fish, once said that the demise of objectivity "relieves me of the obligation to be right . . . and demands only that I be interesting."[11] He now regrets that statement, but he has not disavowed the sentiment. To be sure, what theorists regard as "interesting" may not be what a literate reader, unfamiliar with their arcane language and convoluted reasoning, would find intelligible, let alone interesting. For theorists, what is interesting is what is outré, paradoxical, contradictory, opaque. Since there is no "right" interpretation, the opportunities to be "interesting," in this sense, are unlimited. And since novels and poems are simply "texts" (or "pretexts") that are entirely indeterminate and therefore totally malleable, they can be "textualized," "contextualized," "recontextualized," and "intertextualized" at will. The result is a kind of free-floating verbal association, in which any word or idea can suggest any other (including, or especially, its opposite), and any text can be related in any fashion to any other.

Indeed, the very words of the text are recast, rearranged, and redefined. By the ingenious use of quotation marks, hyphens, diagonals, and parentheses within and around words, by adding or subtracting syllables or letters and crossing out words while keeping them in the text, the critic can elicit the puns, double entendres, paradoxes, ambiguities, and antitheses that testify to the intrinsic "aporia" of language, the infinite play of "*différance*." An English commentator has been moved to observe that ours is "the age of the inverted commas and the erased idea."[12]

In this Aesopian world, Jacques Derrida is free to transmute the philosopher Hegel into the word "Hegel," which evokes the French *aigle*, thus connoting "imperial or historic power."[13] This, in turn, inspires Geoffrey Hartman to identify *aigle* with Nietzsche's *Ekel*, meaning "disgust."[14] By such verbal gymnastics, the critic can engage in the most elaborate contortions and produce the most startling effects, unrestrained by anything but the limits of his own wit and audacity. It is an enviable position in which he finds himself, although not so enviable for the subject of this exercise, the philosopher Hegel, who is so readily reduced to an object of "disgust."

Not all of the practitioners of these arts identify themselves as deconstructionists. Geoffrey Hartman has described himself and Harold Bloom as "barely deconstructionists" compared with those "boa-deconstructors" Derrida, Paul de Man, and J. Hillis Miller.[15] Others have more prosaically distinguished between "soft" and "hard" deconstructionists.

After the revelations about de Man's collaboration with the Nazis, some of the "softer" members of this school defected, denying that they are now, or ever have been, deconstructionists; some profess not to know any deconstructionists. Others stood firm, defending both deconstruction and de Man. Hartman himself took the occasion to offer so "soft" an interpretation of deconstruction—it was essentially, he said, a "defense of literature" and a "critique of German idealism"—that most literary critics might be regarded as unwitting deconstructionists.[16]

That deconstruction is not just a variant of the familiar modes of critical interpretation may be seen by examining one of the best known and most highly regarded examples of this genre: J. Hillis Miller's analysis of one of Wordsworth's "Lucy" poems, "A Slumber Did My Spirit Seal." This essay is especially noteworthy because Miller is one of the most influential figures of this school; because he is so enamored of his reading of this poem that he has repeated it on several occasions; because it has been taken as a model of deconstruction by deconstructionists themselves; and because it ventures to interpret a poem that has been admired by generations of readers and commented on by a host of scholars.[17] Moreover, the poem itself has the virtue of being so brief—only eight short lines—that one can easily keep it in mind as one reads the interpretation.

> *A slumber did my spirit seal;*
> *I had no human fears;*
> *She seemed a thing that could not feel*
> *The touch of earthly years.*
>
> *No motion has she now, no force;*
> *She neither hears nor sees;*

> *Rolled round in earth's diurnal course,*
> *With rocks, and stones, and trees.*

Traditionally the poem has been read as an elegy, a memorial to a girl who died at a tragically young age. Most commentators have dwelt upon what would be obvious to any thoughtful reader—the contrast, for example, between past and present, life and death, the innocence of youth and the tragic sense of mortality that comes with age. Miller finds in it a good many other contrasts, starting with "male as against female" and going on to "mother as against daughter or sister, or perhaps any female family member as against some woman from outside the family, that is, mother, sister, or daughter against mistress or wife, in short, incestuous desires against legitimate sexual feelings." He also brings to bear upon the poem—in accord with the principle that any text is relevant to any other, however far removed in time or subject—such authorities as Walter Benjamin, Paul de Man, Nietzsche, Wallace Stevens, Plato, Thales, and especially Heidegger. Thus Heidegger's play on the word "thing," in his commentary on Plato's *Theaetetus*, is applied to Wordsworth's use of that word. Where the "common reader" might assume that the poem's reference to the girl as a "thing" was meant to emphasize the fact that she was no longer alive, Miller, inspired by Heidegger, explains that "a young girl" (presumably dead or alive) is a thing because "something is missing in her which men have."

But the poem is even "odder" than this, Miller says, as he proceeds to explicate the "obscure sexual drama" played out in it, a drama that has as its source the death of Wordsworth's own mother when he was eight. Lucy represents at the same time "the virgin child and the missing mother," a "virgin 'thing'" who is "sexually penetrated while still remaining virgin." The speaker in the poem is not only the opposite of Lucy—"male to her female, adult knowledge to her prepubertal innocence"; he is also "the displaced representative of both the penetrated and the penetrator." In fact Lucy and the speaker are "the same," though the poet is also "the perpetually excluded difference from Lucy, an unneeded increment, like an abandoned child." Since "Lucy" means ("of course") light, to "possess" Lucy would be to rejoin the "lost source of light"; thus Lucy is also the male principle, the "father sun as logos." To think about Lucy's death is to cause her death, for "thinking recapitulates in reverse mirror image the action of the earthly years in touching, penetrating, possessing, killing, encompassing, turning the other into oneself and therefore being left only with a corpse, an empty sign."

And so the interpretation goes on, becoming more and more convoluted, with Miller finally concluding that he has "seemingly" come far from the subject of his essay, "the state of contemporary literary study." But one might also conclude that he has come even further from those eight delicate lines of the poem.

This exercise in deconstruction recalls an image used by Trilling in another prophetic essay. While literary critics, he said, were endowing literature with "virtually angelic powers," they were also making it clear to the readers of literature that "the one thing you do not do when you meet an angel is wrestle with him."[18] What would he have said of critics today who tell their readers that when you meet an angel, not only do you not wrestle with him, you play with him—play word games with him, play fast and loose with his "text," play havoc with reason, common sense, and emotion? It is ironic, in view of the turgidity of their prose, to find deconstructionists solemnly invoking the principle of *jouissance* or *tromperie*, and to hear Geoffrey Hartman call them, not in criticism but in praise, "clowns or jongleurs."[19]

It is in this spirit, playfully and at the same time ponderously, that deconstructionists summon up the image of the abyss, an abyss that exists for them in language alone. Do we not all experience, Hartman observes, "the fear (a thrilling fear) of the abyss in all words whose resonance haunts us and must be appeased"?[20] The preface to a translation of one of Derrida's works explains: "The fall into the abyss of deconstruction inspires us with as much pleasure as fear. We are intoxicated with the prospect of never hitting bottom."[21] And Paul de Man is described as "the only man who ever looked into the abyss and came away smiling."[22] De Man came away smiling for the same reason that Hartman found the abyss thrilling and Derrida found it pleasurable—because his abyss is a purely linguistic one, constructed entirely out of words—indeed, out of a play on words. And having been so willfully constructed, it can be as willfully reconstructed and deconstructed.

Philosophy also has its abysses, and some philosophers are confronting them in the same way—playfully and irreverently, as a linguistic construct, having no "correspondence" with anything posing as "reality" or "truth." They quote Nietzsche's many maxims on this subject, such as his celebrated one on truth: "Truths are illusions of which one has forgotten that they *are* illusions; worn-out metaphors which have become powerless to affect the senses; coins which have their obverse effaced and now are no longer of account as coins but merely as metal."[23] But there is nothing illusory or metaphoric in Nietzsche's abyss, which is the primal, tragic fact of the human condition. Heidegger's abyss, on the other hand, is to be found in the sentence "Language speaks," and in that abyss one falls not downward but upward; indeed, there one can "become at home, . . . find a residence, a dwelling place for the life of man."[24]

Richard Rorty, one of America's most respected philosophers, calls himself a pragmatist, but so "light-mindededly," as he would say, that one can hardly recognize any kinship with his notably grave progenitor John Dewey. The main principle governing Rorty's philosophy is that there is no fixed or fundamental principle, no "essential" truth or reality. Indeed, philosophy, he says, no longer exists as an independent discipline. Marx promised to abolish philosophy by replacing it with "positive science"—that is, Marxism, which is deemed to be scientific rather than philosophical because it is simply the depiction of "reality."[25] Rorty would abolish philosophy by abolishing reality itself, which is nothing more than the arbitrary construct of the philosopher.

Unlike Marx, Rorty is confident that his revolution is already largely achieved. It is getting more and more difficult, Rorty good-humoredly observes, to locate "a real live metaphysical prig" who thinks there is a "reality" to be explored and a "truth" about reality to be discovered. There are, to be sure, a few such dodoes left.

> You can still find philosophy professors who will solemnly tell you that they are seeking *the truth*, not just a story or a consensus but an honest-to-God, down-home, accurate representation of the way the world is. A few of them will even claim to write in a clear, precise, transparent way, priding themselves on manly straightforwardness, on abjuring "literary" devices.[26]*

---

*This is reminiscent of the much quoted passage in Derrida's "White Mythology," deriding the "metaphysical naivety of the wretched peripatetic" who does not realize that metaphysics is nothing more than mythology:

> A white mythology which assembles and reflects Western culture: the white man takes his own mythology (that is, Indo-European mythology), his *logos*—that is, the *mythos* of

Rorty himself has given up any such old-fashioned "philosophical machismo."[28] He has even gone so far in repudiating "machismo" as to apply the feminine pronoun to the "anti-essentialist" philosopher and the masculine pronoun to the "essentialist"—this after identifying himself as an "anti-essentialist."[29]

Rather than seek an essential truth, Rorty calls upon philosophers to "dream up as many new contexts as possible . . . to be as polymorphous in our adjustments as possible, to recontextualize for the hell of it."[30] They should, in fact, become philosophers-cum-poets, adopting a "light-minded aestheticism" to traditional philosophical questions, for only such an aestheticism can further the "disenchantment of the world." This disenchantment, moreover, must extend itself to morality as well as truth. Just because other people take moral issues seriously does not mean that philosophers should share that seriousness. On the contrary, they should "josh them out of the habit" of being serious and get them to look at moral issues aesthetically, playfully.[31]

"Taking philosophy seriously," Rorty explains, is not only philosophically naïve, positing a reality and a truth that do not exist, but politically dangerous, for essentialism encourages fundamentalism and fanaticism of the kind displayed by Shiites, Marxists, and Nazis. This is Heidegger's great fault. It is not his particular doctrines about the nature of man, reason, or history that are "intrinsically fascistic." Nor are his doctrines invalidated by the fact that he himself was a Nazi, an anti-Semite, and altogether "a rather nasty piece of work." His mistake is rather in thinking that "philosophy must be taken seriously." Rorty warns us against this common mistake. An original philosopher is the product of a "neural kink," and one should no more look to him for

his idiom, for the universal form of that which it is still his inescapable desire to call Reason.[27]

wisdom or virtue than to an original mathematician, micro-biologist, or chess master. Heidegger is an original in this sense, and one should take from him and make of him what one likes—which is not at all, Rorty admits, what Heidegger might have liked. The proper approach to Heidegger is "to read his books as he would not have wished them to be read: in a cool hour, with curiosity, and an open, tolerant mind."[32]

Or perhaps one should read them as novels. If Rorty finds no wisdom in philosophy, he does find it in fiction, which is not burdened by "transcultural notions of validity." Endorsing Milan Kundera's tribute to "the wisdom of the novel," Rorty announces that he happily joins him in "appealing to the novel against philosophy." To be sure, this may have unpleasant consequences, since the "realm of possibility," as revealed in the novel, is unlimited and uncontrolled. Might it not mean, for example, that "the wisdom of the novel encompasses a sense of how Hitler might be seen as in the right and the Jews in the wrong?" Yes, it does, and novels will surely be written that portray Hitler as he saw himself and that persuade readers to sympathize with him. Such novels will be written and *must* be written, Rorty insists, if we are to be faithful, as we should be, to "the wisdom of the novel."[33]

Kundera has not, in fact, written such a novel, and it is unlikely that he would. But Heidegger wrote books and delivered lectures that justified Nazism—and not only early in the Nazi regime but after the war, when the facts of the Holocaust were fully known. In 1948, rebuked by Herbert Marcuse for not recanting his support of the regime or denouncing the extermination of the Jews, Heidegger replied that Hitler's actions were comparable to the measures taken by the Allied forces against the East Germans. The following year he delivered a speech that may be the ultimate in "moral equivalency." "Agriculture," he declared, "is now a motorized food industry, in essence the same as the manufacturing of corpses in the gas chambers and extermination camps, the same as the blockade and starvation of the countryside, the same as the production of the hydrogen bombs."[34]

Looking into the abyss of philosophy, one might say, Heidegger saw the beasts of Nazism and found them tolerable. Rorty looks into the abyss of Heidegger—coolly, curiously, tolerantly—and sees not Heidegger as he saw himself, indeed, as he was, but an "original and interesting writer." Divorced from any "essential" truth, from any practical morality, and from the political consequences of his own philosophy, Heidegger can be readily assimilated into Rorty's philosophy—or non-philosophy. By the same token, we can look into Rorty and see him not as he sees himself—as the only sensible, pragmatic philosopher of liberal democracy—but as the proponent of a relativism-cum-aestheticism that verges on nihilism and that may ultimately subvert liberal democracy together with all the other priggish metaphysical notions about truth, morality, and reality.

So too the discipline of history has more than its share of abysses and still more historians prepared to make of them what they will. Like those literary critics who recontextualize and deconstruct texts, or those philosophers who abolish philosophy and aestheticize morality, so there are historians who propose to "demystify" (and, some might say, "dehistoricize") history. This is the intention behind some of the most fashionable schools of history: that which explains everything in terms of race, class, and gender; that which focuses entirely upon the daily lives of ordinary people ("history from below"); that which "structuralizes" history, displacing individuals, events, and ideas by impersonal structures, forces, and institutions; and that which "deconstructs" it, making all statements about the past aesthetic constructs of the historian.[35]

The effect in each case is to mute the drama of history, to void it of moral content, to mitigate evil and belittle greatness. It is ironic to find these schools flourishing at a time when the reality of history has been all too dramatic, when we have plumbed the depths of degradation and witnessed heroic efforts of redemption. Looking into the most fearsome abysses of modern times, these historians see not beasts but faceless bureaucrats, not corpses but statistics, not willful acts of brutality and murder but the banal routine of everyday life, not gas chambers and gulags but military-industrial-geopolitical complexes.

Of all these schools, history-from-below may seem most innocent. Yet confronted with the abyss, it is as evasive and delusive as the others. If it cannot take the measure of greatness, neither can it appreciate the enormity of evil. *Alltagsgeschichte*, the history of everyday, workaday life, can tell us much about the daily wartime life of ordinary Germans— the way they went about their jobs, struggled to make ends meet, coped with the difficulties of rationing and shortages, sent off husbands and fathers to die abroad, and suffered injuries and deaths from air raids at home. All of this may be true, but it is hardly the whole of the truth or even the most essential part of the truth. Modeled on anthropology, this mode of history professes to be "value-free." The result, one historian has pointed out, is that "workaday life in the Third Reich could be remembered as no more than workaday life."[36] Another explains that it conveys "the normality of a 'normal' German living a 'normal' life," but tells us nothing about the uniqueness—indeed, abnormality—of that time.[37]

Even in what it does tell us, it may be delusive. If ordinary people can give no evidence of the horrors of concentration camps or of deliberate, systematic, massive murders, they may give distorted evidence of those events that were within their daily experience—beatings on the street, children expelled from school, Jews forced from their homes and jobs. Such events may have impinged very little on the consciousness of people preoccupied with their own concerns or, it may be, prepared to ignore or belittle them because they themselves were not averse to them. The historian looking for evidence of anti-Semitism on the part of ordinary people may find only "mild," "passive" anti-Semitism, and will have no way of knowing the effect of such anti-Semitism in sanctioning and thus promoting official, virulent anti-Semitism. Or, finding evidence of a popular belief in eugenics, the historian may subsume that mild anti-Semitism under the larger, "functional" category of eugenics.

The effect of such a history would be to create "a Final Solution with no anti-Semitism; a Holocaust that is not unique."[38] It might even remove Hitler altogether from the social history of the Nazi period. And with Hitler gone, with nothing left but the normal and banal, *Alltagsgeschichte* becomes an "apologia" for Nazism.[39]

The most recent and modish way of demystifying the Holocaust is by "deconstructing" it. In principle, deconstruction is obliged to "problematize" the Holocaust as it does all historical "texts." Because of the sensitivity of the subject, however, and to avoid being identified with the "revisionist" school that denies the reality of the Holocaust, deconstructionists have trod warily.[40] But they have been less reticent when confronted with the revelation that one of their leading lights, Paul de Man, had written anti-Semitic articles in a pro-Nazi journal early in the war. Whether or not those writings by de Man—and, more important, his evasiveness and duplicity on this and related subjects throughout his life—may properly be taken as a reflection on deconstruction itself, there can be little doubt that the responses of his colleagues, some in the form of lengthy essays, are part of the literature of deconstruction. For in rallying to the defense of de Man, as most of them have, they have deconstructed his "texts" much as they might deconstruct any literary, philosophical, or historical text—and have deconstructed his critics as well.

Jacques Derrida's essay on de Man is a classic of this genre. De Man had said that it was a form of "vulgar anti-Semitism" to think that German culture could be identified with Judaism. Derrida interprets this to mean not what a reader of that pro-Nazi journal would surely have taken it to mean—that it was "vulgar" to identify German culture with Judaism—but rather that de Man was condemning "anti-Semitism *itself inasmuch as* [Derrida's italics] it is vulgar, always and essentially vulgar." Having thus absolved de Man of the charge of anti-Semitism, Derrida goes on to accuse de Man's critics (his "prosecutors," Derrida calls them) of being the real culprits—latter-day Nazis, in effect. It is they who reproduce the "exterminating gesture" ("gesture"!) of the Nazis by virtually "censuring [*sic*] or burning" de Man's books, and who speak of him as a "propagator," which is a code word for "censorship" [*sic*] and "denunciation" to the police. It is these critics who are guilty of an "ideologizing moralization" that is "immorality itself." And it is their "war," the war in the press, the war between de Man's critics and his friends, even the war within de Man himself, that is at issue as much as the war against the Nazis. After reading this exercise in deconstruction and apologetics, one can understand Derrida's remark that the overwhelming feeling produced in him by thinking about all this is one of "immense compas-

On Looking into the Abyss / 2 1

sion"—not, as one might think, for the victims of Nazism, but for de Man's "enormous suffering" and "agony."[41]*

Others have been less imaginative in their defense of de Man, excusing him on the grounds of youthful aberration, political expediency, and human frailty. One defender takes comfort in the fact that de Man proposed not the extermination of the Jews but only their expulsion from Europe[43]; another that he was not anti-Semitic but only "intellectually vulgar."[44] Still another reminds us that although many facts about the affair have emerged, facts in themselves are meaningless. "It is all a matter of interpretation, and each interpretation will probably reveal more about the interpreter than about de Man."[45]

Geoffrey Hartman, one of de Man's most devoted admirers (and himself, as he points out, a refugee from Nazi Germany), is pained by de Man's behavior, but finds "the American reaction, in its rush to judgment, as hard to take as the original revelations."[46] He also finds that those revelations, seen in perspective, are not quite so bad as we might think. De Man's writings were anti-Semitic, to be sure, but not a "vulgar" anti-Semitism, at least "not by the terrible standards of the day"; and his comments on the "Jewish problem" were "mild" compared with the "vicious" propaganda in other papers. De Man was only part of a larger problem. His "dirty secret" was the "dirty secret of a good

---

*Derrida has responded to the revelations about Heidegger's Nazism in a similar spirit of compassion. Heidegger, he explains, had been briefly taken in by Nazism because of a philosophical error on his part, a misguided subjectivism and "metaphysical humanism." As for Heidegger's later silence on the Holocaust, this too Derrida finds defensible. Instead, Derrida reserves his criticism for those who are quick to condemn the silence; it is they who are "a bit indecent, even obscene."[42]

part of civilized Europe," so that "once again," Hartman observes, speaking for all of us, "we feel betrayed by the intellectuals." And if de Man himself chose not to reveal that secret and never to acknowledge his past, it was because to do so would be an "effort of exculpation," thus a repetition of the original "error." What he did instead was to devote himself to his lifework, a critique of the "rhetoric of totalitarianism," the tendency to "totalize" language and literature. And this, Hartman concludes, "looks like a belated, but still powerful, act of conscience."[47]*

If the defense of de Man often reads like a defense of deconstruction itself, it also resorts to arguments that clearly violate the principles of deconstruction. Thus his critics are taken to task for failing to consider his "authorial intentions," the historical and biographical context of his articles, even the testimony of his acquaintances. J. Hillis Miller invokes some of these arguments, going so far as to accuse the critics of doing great damage to "the possibilities of rational and informed discussion."[49] Similarly, Derrida, claiming to find factual errors in one critical article, "shudders to think

---

*Another colleague and disciple of de Man, Shoshana Felman, explains why his silence, his refusal to confess, was itself an ethical statement.

> In the testimony of a work that performs actively an exercise of silence not as simple silence but as the absolute refusal of any trivializing or legitimizing discourse (of apology, of narrative, or of psychologizing explanation of recent history), de Man articulates . . . the incapacity of apologetic discourse to account for history as Holocaust, the ethical impossibility of a *confession that, historically and philosophically, cannot take place.* This complex articulation of the impossibility of concession embodies, paradoxically enough, not a denial of the author's guilt but, on the contrary, the most radical and irrevocable assumption of historical responsibility.[48]

that its author teaches history at a university."[50] If one is surprised to hear such conventional sentiments from theorists who normally deride "facticity" and rationality, "authorial intentions" and "extralinguistic" contexts, one may also recall their contempt for the "linear logic" that would preclude such inconsistency. (One may also sympathize with Miller, who was unfortunate enough to publish a book, the same year as the revelations about de Man appeared, predicting that "the millennium of universal justice and peace" would come "if all men and women became good readers in de Man's sense."[51]

The de Man case has many parallels to an earlier controversy about a book by David Abraham on the background of Nazism.[52] One of the points of criticism concerns the dedication, which reads, "For my parents—who at Auschwitz and elsewhere suffered the worst consequences of what I can merely write about."[53] A naïve reader might suppose that the "worst consequences" suffered by Abraham's parents, as by so many others at Auschwitz and elsewhere, was death. In fact, his parents were alive when the book was published. The historian Natalie Zemon Davis has analyzed the dedication, defending Abraham against any imputation of deception. In a thousand words she deconstructs and reconstructs the nineteen-word dedication so that it becomes a tribute not to dead parents but to live ones—and a tribute as well to the "survivors' son," the dedicator, who penetrated to a deeper truth than appears on the surface.[54]

Davis explains why the superficial reading of the dedication is erroneous. Few readers, she says, are likely to interpret it as a dedication to the dead, since one cannot dedicate anything to the dead, but only to their memory; moreover, the book jacket identifies the author as an assistant professor at Princeton, suggesting that he was too young to be the son of parents who perished in the camps. The dedication is properly read as an expression of thanks to the author's parents and as a reminder of "their special relation to his subject matter." While the book itself says almost nothing about anti-Semitism—it is a "structural analysis" of the roots of Nazism, Davis explains, and therefore deals with impersonal "social forces"—the last line of the book "circles round to the 'consequences' of the dedication" by referring to the German businessmen who "paved the road to serfdom" with "gold and blood." The dedication is thus a "strategy" by which the author reclaims the past. "So that's how it happened, says the survivors' son [or so Davis has him saying]; not the work of devils, but of historical forces and actors." This is the message of the dedication: "turn suffering into writing and figuring out, inform accusations with understanding, let the tragic endings of 'gold and blood' not be the last word."[55]

One's admiration for the creativity of this exercise is tempered by the realization of how far it has gone from the "text" itself—from the implied death of the author's parents to their resurrection as survivors; from the "worst consequences" inflicted by the Nazis in the death camps to the Weimar businessmen who "paved the road to serfdom" (as if "serfdom" is equivalent to the Holocaust); and from the Holocaust itself seen as deliberate, premeditated evil ("the work of devils") to an "understanding" of it as the product of "historical forces and actors." One may well be dismayed by the expenditure of so much ingenuity on a subject as solemn and unambiguous as this, an all too real abyss in which millions of people did in fact suffer the "worst consequences."

The implications of this mode of thought, exhibited in the writing and teaching of some of our most eminent literary critics, philosophers, and historians, have not been fully appreciated. (At least three of the writers who feature prominently in this essay—J. Hillis Miller, Richard Rorty, and Natalie Zemon Davis—have been presidents of their professional associations.) What happens to our passion for literature when any "text" qualifies as literature, when theory is elevated above poetry and the critic above the poet, and when literature, interpretation, and theory alike are said to be indeterminate and infinitely malleable? What happens to our respect for philosophy—the "love of wisdom," as it once was—when we are told that philosophy has nothing to do with either wisdom or virtue, that what passes as metaphysics is really linguistics, that morality is a form of aesthetics, and that the best thing we can do is not to take philosophy seriously? And what happens to our sense of the past when we are told that there is no past save that which the historian creates; or to our perception of the momentousness of history when we are assured that it is *we* who give moment to history; or to that most momentous historical event, the Holocaust, when it can be so readily "demystified" and "normalized," "structuralized" and "deconstructed"? And what happens when we look into the abyss and see no real beasts but only a pale reflection of ourselves—of our particular race, class, and gender; or, worse yet, when we see only the metaphorical, rhetorical, mythical, linguistic, semiotic, figurative, fictive simulations of our imaginations? And when, looking at an abyss so remote from reality, we are moved to say, like Trilling's students, "How interesting, how exciting."

When Nietzsche looked into the abyss, he saw not only real beasts but the beast in himself. "He who fights with monsters," he warned his reader, "should be careful lest he thereby become a monster. And if thou gaze long into an abyss, the abyss will also gaze into thee."[56] This was all too prophetic, for a few years later the abyss did gaze back at him and drew him down into the depths of insanity. Our professors look into the abyss secure in their tenured positions, risking nothing and seeking nothing save another learned article.

Nietzsche is now a darling of the academy. I have seen T-shirts emblazoned with the slogan "Nietzsche is Peachy." Nietzsche, who had no high regard for the academy but did have a highly developed sense of irony, would have enjoyed that sight.

II

Of Heroes, Villains, and Valets

"NO MAN IS A HERO to his valet." The dictum
has been attributed to Madame de Sévigné in the reign of
Louis XIV.[1] Hegel amplified it to read: "No man is a hero
to his valet; not, however, because the man is not a hero, but
because the valet—is a valet."[2]

This emended version of the proverb first appeared in
1807 in Hegel's *Phenomenology of Spirit* and was later repeated
in his *Philosophy of History* (where he took the occasion to
remind his readers that it was he who coined it, not Goethe,
who had been given credit for it). Hegel had a proprietary
interest in heroes because they were the "world-historical
individuals" whom he saw as the crucial agents in the progress of history. By the same token, he had contempt for
those small-minded men, men with the souls of valets, who
reduce historical individuals to their own level of sensibility
and consciousness.

What pedagogue has not demonstrated of Alexander the Great, of Julius Caesar, that they were instigated by such passions [for conquest and fame] and were consequently immoral men?—whence the conclusion immediately follows that he, the pedagogue, is a better man than they, because he has no such passions; a proof of which lies in the fact that he does not conquer Asia, vanquish Darius and Porus, but while he enjoys life himself, lets others enjoy it too.[3]

The pedagogue looks at a historical figure and sees only a private person. He is like the valet who "takes off the hero's boots, assists him to bed, knows that he prefers champagne, etc."—and knows nothing more about him. "Historical personages waited upon in historical literature by such psychological valets come poorly off; they are brought down by these their attendants to a level with—or rather a few degrees below the level of—the morality of such exquisite discerners of spirit."[4]*

Hegel's pedagogues are our professors. They are the academic critics who treat the masters of literature with all the reverence of a valet, who put Shakespeare to bed, so to speak, remove his boots, take off his clothes, tuck him in, secure in the knowledge that he is only a man like themselves, and that they can read, interpret, and "deconstruct" his plays as if they had written them—as if, to use the current jargon, he is no more "privileged" than they, as if his "authorial voice" has no more "authority" than the voice of the

---

*In the *Phenomenology*, the same point is made in a somewhat different form. There the hero is identified with the "universal" aspect of an action, and the valet with the "individual," "particular," or "personal" aspect. The consciousness that recognizes the personal rather than the universal plays "the part of the *moral* valet towards the agent."[5]

critic. We may also find Hegel's schoolmasters among those historians who look for the essence of history not in the great events of public life but in the small events of private life, who reduce public figures to the level of private persons, who recognize no statesmen but only politicians, who see no "universals" in public affairs but only "particulars," no principles but only self-serving interests.

One can appreciate Hegel's distinction between heroes and valets without being quite so enthusiastic about some of his heroes.* Hegel himself does not absolve his heroes of immorality. "World-historical individuals," he says, are not very considerate of those who stand in their way. They are likely to "trample down many an innocent flower, crush to pieces many an object" in their path. And for this they are indeed subject to "moral reprehension." They are also subject to the misfortunes that commonly befall great men. They die young, like Alexander, or are murdered, like Caesar, or end their lives in exile, like Napoleon. They are not, in fact, happy men—which may be of some consolation, Hegel observes, to those lesser, envious men who are "vexed at what is great and transcendent" and can only belittle and criticize it.[7]

It may also be of some consolation to know, as Hegel tells us elsewhere, that his kind of hero, the "world-historical

---

*Or quite so disparaging of his valets. A reader of this essay rebuked me for maligning valets, for assuming that in serving their masters they were reducing them to their own level rather than according them the respect and dignity proper to a hero. I also stand corrected by Byron, who made it a measure of the true hero that even his valet knew him as such: "In short, he was a perfect cavaliero, / And to his very valet seemed a hero."[6] I hereby apologize to all valets (if there still be such). I use the term metaphorically, not literally. Real valets may be rare, but valet-like souls, unhappily, are not.

individual," is a thing of the past. "Once the state has been founded, there can no longer be any heroes. They come on the scene only in uncivilized conditions."[8] Believing England to be the most modern as well as one of the most civilized of countries, Hegel would not have expected to find heroes there. But he might have found a species of hero in the Eminent Victorians—a modern, civilized, Anglicized version of the hero.

The Eminent Victorians were not Hegelian heroes, and still less, for all their admiration of antiquity, Greek heroes. They would have thought it presumptuous to claim for themselves, or to have others claim on their behalf, the quality of "greatness of soul" (*megalopsychia*) that Aristotle attributed to the hero. Nor did they aspire to be world-historical individuals changing the destiny of mankind. What they did have, however, was an individuality and "high-mindedness" (curiously, the English term used for *megalopsychia* in a recent translation of Aristotle),[9] a force of character and mind, that made them heroic in the eyes of most of their contemporaries—and that made them, like heroes everywhere, the targets of the "pedagogues" of their own time and of later times.

Lord Byron was one such hero—not, properly speaking, a Victorian, having died before the queen ascended the throne, but one of the authentic heroes of Victorian England—indeed, the prototype of the "Byronic hero." His friend Thomas Moore (himself a popular third-rate poet) survived him long enough to write his biography in the form of an annotated edition of Byron's letters and journals. Moore was candid with his readers: "[We] contemplate with pleasure," he told them, "a great mind in its undress, and . . . rejoice in the discovery, so consoling to human pride, that even the mightiest, in their moments of ease and weakness, resemble ourselves."[10] Having undressed Byron and discovered him to resemble himself, Moore found it easy to revise and rearrange Byron's letters and journals for his own literary purposes. At one point he informed his publisher that he was getting on very well with the biography. By omitting an important letter, he eliminated one of Byron's affairs, "making a love the less," as he put it; and by redating another affair, he transferred it from the period when it actually occurred to an earlier period, where it was more "consistent" with his own account.[11] One wonders what Moore would have made of Byron's incestuous relationship with his half sister, had he known of it. When that affair was revealed forty years later, it created a sensation. Tennyson was moved to protest: "What business has the public to want to know all about Byron's wildnesses? He has given them fine work, and they ought to be satisfied."[12]

Tennyson unwittingly pointed to the crucial difference between Victorian biographies and later ones. The Victorians, even while relishing the scandals about their heroes, knew them to be scandals about their *lives*, not about their *work*. Byron's poetry was not thought to be less great because his morals were less than admirable. Nor were George Eliot's novels tainted by her long-standing extramarital affair with George Lewes. Nor was John Stuart Mill's philosophy discredited by his relationship with his great and good friend Harriet for the twenty years while she was still Mrs. John Taylor. Nor was Carlyle's reputation as a moralist diminished by the revelations of his sexual "irregularities," as the Victorians delicately put it. Nor was Gladstone's political career jeopardized by his well-known habit of prowling the streets at night, seeking out prostitutes and lecturing them on the evils of their ways, sometimes bringing them home, where his wife dutifully served them tea—or hot chocolate, according to some accounts.

. . .

The case of Carlyle is the most interesting of these, because he was not only himself a hero, in the Victorian sense of that word; he was also a great celebrator of the hero. His *On Heroes, Hero-Worship and the Heroic in History* defines "hero-worship" as the "reverence and obedience due to men really great and wise," and discourses on the different varieties of heroes: the hero as god, as prophet, as priest, as king, as poet, as man of letters.[13] Like Hegel before him (but without attributing it to Hegel or, for that matter, to Goethe, of whom he was a great admirer), he quoted the adage "No man is a hero to his valet," adding that if the valet "does not know a hero when he sees him," it is because he has a "mean valet-soul."[14] Unable to abide the idea of greatness, the valet can only cut down the hero to his own size. "Show our critics a great man," Carlyle observed, "a Luther for example, [and] they begin to what they call 'account' for him; not to worship him, but take the dimensions of him—and bring him out to be a little kind of man."[15]

Carlyle's hero is a hero, not a saint—a hero to be revered for his greatness and wisdom, whatever his personal foibles and follies. Moreover, the hero is hero enough to withstand the revelations of those foibles and follies. When Sir Walter Scott's biographer John Lockhart was criticized for recounting some unsavory details about the novelist's life, Carlyle defended Lockhart and took the occasion to deride the more timid biographer who would try to make of his hero a paragon of virtue. "How delicate, decent, is English biography," Carlyle jeered, "bless its mealy mouth!" Such a biography is unworthy of its subject, he insisted, because it produces not the portrait of a real live hero, but rather a "white, stainless, impersonal ghost hero." Nor is it worthy of the biographer. "To produce not things, but the ghosts of things, can never be the duty of man."[16]

Carlyle's own biographer, James Anthony Froude, quoted this review at length in the preface to his own work in order to disarm the criticism he anticipated for revealing some unflattering aspects of his subject's marital life. Carlyle himself, perhaps unwittingly, conspired in that revelation when he wrote but did not publish his *Reminiscences,* and then left the manuscript to Froude as his literary executor, with permission to use it as he liked. The only details Froude withheld from his biography were an account of Carlyle's physical abuse of his wife and the rumors that their marriage was unconsummated. These emerged when Froude wrote but did not publish another book on Carlyle, bequeathing *that* manuscript to his own children with instructions to destroy it, together with all his other papers and letters. His instructions, needless to say, were ignored, and the book was published.*

The Victorian biographers, then (at least the best of them), were not nearly as mealymouthed as Carlyle suggested. Their heroes had feet of clay; but they were heroes nonetheless, because their heroism lay not in their feet (or in other lowly organs) but in their minds and works. Froude never intimated, and his readers never assumed, that Carlyle was less a sage because he was, in a sense, less a man. John Morley, a worthy if not quite eminent Victorian, wrote in his biography of Voltaire, apropos a not altogether creditable event in Voltaire's life, "Alas, why after all should men . . . be so cheerfully ready to contemplate the hinder parts of their divinities?"[17] The answer, of course, is that it is all too human to do so, as it is all too human of divi-

---

*It is now generally believed that the rumors were exaggerated, that the marriage was not literally unconsummated although it was certainly unfulfilled. A curious sequel to this story has John Ruskin defending Froude's report of the rumors—curious because of Ruskin's own unconsummated marriage.

nities—human, not godly, divinities—to have such hinder parts. But it is also human, if Carlyle is to be believed, for men to revere such divinities for those qualities that make them divine—or, as we say of mortals rather than gods, to revere heroes for those qualities that make them heroic.

Virginia Woolf once said, only semi-facetiously, "In or about December 1910, human character changed."[18] That is the date of the Postimpressionist exhibition in London that had so momentous an effect on modern art and, she believed, on the modern novel. A comparable change in the character of biography, she suggested elsewhere, occurred in March 1918, when her great friend Lytton Strachey published *Eminent Victorians*.

For Woolf this was the prototype of the "new biography," a biography that for the first time provides the kind of "authentic information" that reveals the real subject: "When and where did the real man live; how did he look; did he wear laced boots or elastic-sided; who were his aunts, and his friends; how did he blow his nose; whom did he love, and how; and when he came to die did he die in his bed like a Christian, or. . . ."[19] The sentence is incomplete, but it is clear that Woolf, and certainly Strachey, thought it likely that he had not died like a Christian—and certainly that he had not lived like a hero.

If the subject of the new biography has become less of a hero, the biographer himself has become more of a hero.

> He [the biographer] is no longer the serious and sympathetic companion, toiling even slavishly in the footsteps of his hero. Whether friend or enemy, admiring or critical, he is an equal. . . . Raised upon a little eminence which his independence has made for him, he sees his

subject spread about him. He chooses; he synthesizes; in short, he has ceased to be the chronicler; he has become an artist.[20]

Thus, while the subject is portrayed as a "real man," a man blowing his nose, wearing boots of a particular kind, making love in a particular manner (the latter being of special interest to Woolf and her Bloomsbury friends), the biographer is elevated to the rank of "artist." The biographer is more than the equal of his subject; he is his superior. "Raised upon a little eminence," as Woolf says, he can look down upon his subject, the better to observe his petty, all too human features.

Virginia Woolf perfectly catches the distinctive quality of the new biography, the reversal of roles by which the ostensible hero, the subject, becomes the valet, and the biographer the hero. From his own position of artistic "eminence," Strachey was privileged to belittle and deride his "Eminent Victorians." Proposing a toast to his own book, he recalled a remark made by another biographer: "When I hear men called 'judicious,' I suspect them; but when I hear them called 'judicious and venerable,' I know they are scoundrels." Strachey amended this to describe his own credo: "When I hear people called 'Victorians,' I suspect them. But when I hear them called 'Eminent Victorians,' I write their lives."[21]

Strachey wrote their lives to discredit them, to reveal the private selves behind the public façades, the private vices that are presumed to belie their public virtues. With great artistic skill, he cuts his heroes down to size—literally in the case of Thomas Arnold, the famous headmaster of Rugby, whose legs are said to be "shorter than they should have been"—a malicious (and probably false) comment on the proponent of "Muscular Christianity."[22] Or the scene is set in such a way as to belittle them: General Gordon, martyr of the siege of Khartoum, is depicted seated at a table on which there are "an open Bible and an open bottle of brandy."[23] Or rhetorical stratagems are used for satirical effect: Cardinal Newman's edition of the *Lives of the Saints* includes biographies, we are told, of Saint Bega, Saint Adamnan, Saint Gundleus, Saint Guthlake, Brother Drithelm, Saint Amphibalus, Saint Wulstan, Saint Ebba, Saint Neot, Saint Ninian, and Cunibert the Hermit—the enumeration of all those unfamiliar names making a mockery of the very idea of sainthood.[24] Or their enthusiasms are ridiculed: Florence Nightingale is given to "morbid longings" for God, a God who is a "glorified sanitary engineer"; she could hardly distinguish between "the Deity and the Drains."[25]

In each case, Strachey exposes not only the "hinder parts" of his subjects but their higher parts, their vital organs, the very qualities that made them heroes. This is the great difference between Victorian biography and the "new biography." The Victorians humanized their heroes, revealed their private vices without denying their public virtues. The new biographers reveal their vices (or more often follies) to dishonor them—to make anti-heroes of them.

Yet even anti-heroes have some vestigial quality of the heroic. They are, at the very least, recognizable individuals. The Eminent Victorians, as Strachey portrays them, are caricatures, objects of mockery, but they retain some lingering traces of eminence, if only by virtue of their individuality; indeed, his caricatures sometimes have the effect of making his subjects seem more individualistic, more distinctive, than they actually were. It remained for the "new history" to complete the task of the "new biography," eliminating those last remnants of heroism by denying not only the idea of eminence but the very idea of individuality.

Two years after Strachey's book appeared, H. G. Wells introduced to England the "new history" that had emerged earlier in the United States.[26] His best-selling *Outline of History* defines history as "the common adventure of all mankind," and describes itself as a work that is not only *about* the "common man" but also *for* the common man; the common man is both its subject and its ideal reader. In his history, Wells promises, a so-called "world-historical" individual like Napoleon will be seen in proper perspective, strutting upon the crest of history like a "cockerel on a dunghill."[27]

Wells's comment on Napoleon epitomizes the double agenda of the new history: to discredit those individuals who have traditionally been identified as the heroes, or "great men," of history; and to replace them by the "common man"—or (if this term sounds invidious or sexist) by the "ordinary people," the "anonymous masses." The first part of this agenda has recently acquired the name "pathography," a biography emphasizing the pathological or diseased qualities of the subject—the reverse of "hagiography."[28] And the second goes by the name of "history from below," the history of ordinary people in the ordinary, daily activities of their lives.

By now the new history threatens to displace not only world-historical individuals like Napoleon but all "elitist" figures, the word applied to presidents as well as kings, working-class leaders as well as aristocrats—all those who stand out from the anonymous masses simply by virtue of their *not* being anonymous, their having individual, recognizable identities, with distinctive roles and accomplishments. Only thus, we are told, can we rescue the poor, anonymous masses from "the enormous condescension of posterity."[29] Moreover, it is not only elitist individuals who are disparaged and displaced; it is elitist themes—the great events of history in which individuals necessarily figure prominently, and the great ideas and books that are the products of great minds.*

How can one quarrel with such a worthy purpose? Why should one not want to enlarge and deepen the scope of history by recovering the memory of those who have been forgotten? No sensible person, certainly no conscientious historian, would object to that. One might, however, reasonably object when the suspicion of elitist history leads to the exclusion or belittling of subjects—great figures, great events, great ideas—that actually determined the course of history, for *all* people. Commenting on the tendency among some historians to denigrate the character and achievements of Winston Churchill, G. R. Elton turns the tables on them:

> When I meet a historian who cannot think that there have been great men, great men moreover in politics, I feel myself in the presence of a bad historian; and there are times when I incline to judge all historians by their opinion of Winston Churchill—whether they can see that, no matter how much better the details, often damaging, of man and career become known, he still remains, quite simply, a great man.[31]

---

*In America this has expressed itself in the recent "revisionist" views of Columbus, in which the "discovery" of America was first downgraded to an "encounter" and then vilified as an "invasion" and "depredation." In England a similar process has taken place in regard to the Armada. The reviewer of several works published on the occasion of its four-hundredth anniversary remarks that whatever epic dimension is left to that event is reserved to the defeated Spanish fleet on its terrible voyage home. He relates hearing someone say, "1588, when we *used* to think we defeated the Spaniards."[30]

One might also object when history-from-below itself becomes an exercise in condescension—when the historian denies to the ordinary people ideas, motives, and interests over and above the ordinary concerns of their daily lives. For it is then not only the historian who is reduced to the level of valet, who cannot see anything heroic in history; it is also the people who are reduced to that level, who are denied any aspect of the heroic, any connection with a "universal consciousness," as Hegel would say, an order of being that elevates them above the immediate, mundane, particular circumstances of their lives.

This point was brought vividly home to me a few years ago when I wrote an essay arguing that the great political events of history were not only important in themselves but were important to the ordinary people of the time and, indeed, were of great interest to those people. Among my critics was a well-known social historian who protested that political affairs were, and still are, of little concern to ordinary people. Surely, he said, the vast majority of people have always thought that "where they lived and how they made a living, who they married, and what happened to their children" were far more important than "who won the last election."[32] I was struck by the unwitting arrogance (elitism, one might say) of that comment—as if only a Harvard professor could be expected to care about his job, home, and children, and also about the last election.

The latest display of this professional deformation is the attack on the "canon" on the grounds that it is dominated by "Dead White Males"—"DWMs," or "Dweems," as they are familiarly known. I was introduced to a variation on this term—"BGs," "Big Guys"—by the head of the women's studies program in a distinguished college, who explained that the problem is not only that these Big Guys are Guys, but that they are Big, thus "privileging," as she put it, great books, ideas, and events—and, worse, privileging the very idea of greatness, of genius, of the unique person seeking transcendent truths that are presumed to have enduring value. This idea itself—that there is such a thing as greatness, genius, uniqueness, that people should celebrate and aspire to such qualities, that there are truths that transcend race, gender, and class, and that all people, even ordinary people, can share in such truths and be elevated by them—all of this, she insisted, is a peculiarly masculine idea. And it can only be rectified by creating a feminist "counter-canon" representing women who embody peculiarly feminine values—women poets who say "I'm not creating this poem for eternity," and women writers who say "I don't want to celebrate transcendent truths, I want to celebrate the little things in women's lives . . . the small nurturing things that women do."

I would like to think that this is an extreme attitude, that most feminists do not want to replace the canon of BGs, Big Guys, with a counter-canon of LGs, Little Gals. But the presumption against greatness goes deep. It is, in fact, at the heart of the debate about "great books." The argument is no longer about the composition of the canon, whether it is adequately representative of race, gender, and class, but about the very idea of greatness, a greatness that traditionally has been thought to transcend race, gender, and class. And about genre too, for this also is a subject of contention. It can no longer be taken for granted that Milton deserves to be more "privileged" than Mickey Mouse, that high culture is higher, more elevating, than popular culture, and that some events in history are more momentous than others.

The feminist who would relegate women to the "little things" of life—consigning them, an old-fashioned feminist might say, to the kitchen—is diminishing and trivializing their lives, as surely as the social historian who assumes that ordinary people are indifferent to politics, to public affairs beyond the province of their daily lives. Even Hegel, not noted for his democratic proclivities, gave the ordinary people more credit than that. Most people, he agreed, are immersed in the particularities of their lives, but all of them have access to the "universal"; they partake of the universal by virtue of their membership in the state, whose laws and institutions transcend the particular and give them a role in the evolving course of history.

Hegel would have been pleased, I like to think, with a recent television production dramatizing the American Civil War which captures this sense of transcendence. Apart from being a gripping and remarkably accurate historical narrative, the film exemplifies the heroic nature of a great event, one whose greatness is as evident today as it was at the time, despite the commonplace brutalities of the war itself—the muck and muddle of battlefields, of generals competent and incompetent, of soldiers maimed and dying. For all of that, the Civil War was, from beginning to end, a great national, political, social, and moral experience, which can only be understood (as the film makes clear) by a skillful combination of history-from-above and history-from-below—the magnificent rhetoric of Lincoln's speeches complementing the homely and equally moving rhetoric of soldiers' letters to their wives. It was a truly noble event in which privates in the army and newly liberated slaves were as much the heroes as generals and statesmen, partaking in the "universal," as Hegel would have said, and being elevated by that universality even, unhappily, as it often destroyed them.[33]

The problem with a valet-like conception of history is not only its denigration of greatness and heroism but also its denigration of individuality and freedom. A century and a half ago, Alexis de Tocqueville anticipated just this problem. In a remarkably prescient and very brief chapter (only three or four pages) of *Democracy in America*, entitled "Some Characteristics Peculiar to Historians in Democratic Centuries," Tocqueville pointed to the essential distinction between the old history and the new. In aristocratic periods, he explained, historians tend to "attribute everything that happens to the will and character of particular men," and to assume "slight accidents to be the cause of the greatest revolutions." In democratic periods, on the other hand, they tend to "attribute hardly any influence over the destinies of mankind to individuals," and to make "general causes responsible for the smallest particular events." The danger of the democratic mode was that in belittling or ignoring "individual will" in the making of history, the historian also belittles "human freedom."

A cause so vast that it acts at the same time on millions of men, and so strong that it bends them all together in the same direction, may easily seem irresistible. Seeing that one does yield to it, one is very near believing that one cannot stand up to it.

Thus historians who live in democratic times do not only refuse to admit that some citizens may influence the destiny of a people, but also take away from the people themselves the faculty of modifying their own lot and make them depend either on an inflexible providence or on a kind of blind fatality.[34]

Tocqueville's remarks apply to determinisms of every kind: the economic determinism of Marxism, the geographic and demographic determinism of the early *Annaliste* historians, the sociological determinism that makes of people the "products" of their society, or the currently popular determinism that defines them in terms of their race, class, and gender. Each has the effect of belittling the will, ideas, actions, and freedom of individuals. Today more than ever we have reason to heed Tocqueville's words: "It is important not to let this idea [free will] grow dim, for we need to raise men's souls, not to complete their prostration."[35]

Without will, without individuals, there are no heroes. But neither are there villains. And the absence of villains is as prostrating, as soul-destroying, as the absence of heroes. About the same time that Madame de Sévigné is said to have coined the aphorism "No man is a hero to his valet," another French notable, La Rochefoucauld, enunciated another important truth: "There are heroes of evil as well as of good." The two maxims may be amalgamated: "No man is a hero to his valet, and no man is a villain to his valet." To the valet, the master is a man like all men, someone whose boots have to be removed, who has to be helped into bed, who has a taste for champagne. The valet may even know other things about him, that he is a good or bad master or husband or father. What the valet will not know is whether he is a hero or a villain—a great statesman or philosopher, or, it may be, a tyrant or charlatan.

Nor will the historian know these things if he adheres to the mode of history known as structuralism (or functionalism, as it is sometimes called). For the structuralist, the decisive facts about Nazism, for example, are not the ideas, policies, or even actions of Hitler and the Nazis, but the structure of the German state, the nature of its bureaucracy and pressure groups, the exigencies of economics and geography.[36] The effect of this structuralist analysis is as Tocqueville predicted. To depreciate the importance of individuals, ideas, and will is to belittle the role of Hitler and the Nazi leaders, to minimize or even deny their avowed intentions of conquest and mass murder, and to evade the issue of evil. As Lucy Dawidowicz, the preeminent historian of the Holocaust, put it: "The structuralists have thus eliminated the exercise of free will in human society and deprived men and women of their capacity to choose between good and evil."[37]

To "structuralize" Nazism is to trivialize and "de-moralize" it, to make evil banal. It is also to "de-historicize" it, to belie the facts of history. The ideas and intentions, the willful policies and actions of Nazis are surely as much the reality of history as the structure of the state, of peer groups and bureaucracies, of social, economic, and geomilitary forces. Even to understand the "unanticipated consequences" of ideas and policies, it is necessary to understand the ideas and policies that gave rise to those consequences. Structuralists criticize traditional historians of Nazism for the fallacy, as they see it, of "personalizing" history—as if one of the basic principles of Nazism were not the "Führer principle," deifying precisely the person of Hitler. Or they charge these historians with the fallacy of "intentionalism"—as if Hitler had not publicly announced his intentions and as if those intentions were not literally, all too literally, executed.[38]

The same analysis has been applied to the history of the Soviet Union under Stalin. The structuralists do not see Stalinism as a form of totalitarianism, a tyranny imposed by the Stalinist regime in accord with Communist ideology. Indeed, they deny that either the regime or the ideology was responsible for most of the events of that time. The policies and actions associated with Stalin, such as the purges, are said to have been largely improvised, a response to "spontaneous" pressures from "social constituencies" below, rather than a deliberate strategy devised and implemented by the regime above. On this interpretation, Stalin himself is described as coming to power on a wave of "cultural revolution from below" reflecting the popular desire for "social mobility" and "democratization."[39] Or such unfortunate episodes as the famine, collectivization, and "de-kulakization" are attributed to impersonal "sociopolitical and economic" forces and to the "complex webs of industrialization and state-building," the result of "normal, rational processes" inherent in modernity itself.[40]

The structuralist interpretation, according to the new "cohort" of historians (as they refer to themselves), has the salutary effect of undermining "the totalitarian model of the Stalinist system to the point where it is no longer worth using."[41] One historian explains that such concepts as "totalitarianism" and "the terror" are obsolete because they are the products of the Cold War mentality, the anti-Communist hysteria that infected the older scholars. Another finds them objectionable because they are moral judgments, and "judging Stalin" is an "exercise in moral imperialism."[42] Because structuralism eschews such moral judgments, it alone is said to provide an objective view of the Soviet Union.

Robert Conquest, who has conclusively documented the facts about Soviet totalitarianism and the terror, describes this effort to portray "the Stalin period without Stalinism" as equivalent not just to *Hamlet* without the Prince, but *Hamlet* with no characters at all, "only the scenery and a voice off chanting, 'There's something sociologically interesting in the state of Denmark.' "[43] Another historian explains why it is precisely for reasons of objectivity that historians must confront the nature of the Stalinist regime, a regime that was essentially and intentionally, not accidentally or incidentally, totalitarian and terroristic.

> Historians must write about the terror not in order to vent their indignation, but because that subject is essential to our understanding of absolutely every aspect of Soviet life in the 1930s. Terror was not an epi-

phenomenon. It is not a topic like the history of Soviet sports or Soviet opera. Because of the terror, parents talked differently to their children, writers wrote differently, workers and managers talked to one another differently. . . . Because of the terror, millions perished. . . . Whatever topics we choose, we cannot get away from the fact that those were murderous times and Stalinism was a murderous system.[44]

Among younger historians especially, who like to think of themselves as being on the "cutting edge" of the discipline, the structuralist interpretation is seductive. To be sure, now that Russian historians are revealing the murderous facts of the Communist regime and confirming Conquest's estimates about the extent of "The Great Terror," it is becoming more difficult for American historians, however sophisticated, to ignore those facts. It may even be that the word "terror" will be rehabilitated, and that "totalitarian"—"a term long out of vogue in American academia," one historian said only a few years ago[45]—will return to fashion.

That may happen, but one cannot be confident that it will. An ingenious historian can always find ways of eluding reality. One such historian is Fernand Braudel, the most influential member of the French structuralist school of Annalistes. His seminal work, *The Mediterranean in the Time of Philip II*, exemplifies the theory that long-term, inanimate, impersonal forces—geography, demography, ecology, economics—are the "deeper realities" of history, in contrast to short-term events, which are ephemeral and superficial. For Braudel, these short-term events include not only the wars and conquests of Philip's reign but also such "events" (or "conjunctures," Braudel calls them) as the Inquisition and the Renaissance. In a memorable passage, Braudel compares these ephemeral events to fireflies that glow briefly in the night and quickly disappear, leaving behind no illumination, no trace of their existence.[46]

Braudel's book is an extraordinary feat of scholarship, if only because he wrote it from memory, without benefit of libraries or archives, while he was in a prisoner-of-war camp in Germany during World War II. He later recalled the temper of mind in which he had written it: it was, he said, "a direct existential response to the tragic times I was passing through."

> All those occurrences which poured in upon us from the radio and the newspapers of our enemies, or even the news from London which our clandestine receivers gave us—I had to outdistance, reject, deny them. Down with occurrences, especially vexing ones! I had to believe that history, destiny, was written at a much more profound level.[47]

The "occurrences" that Braudel sought to "outdistance, reject, deny" were nothing less than one of the most devastating wars in modern history and one of the most catastrophic events of all times, the Holocaust, both of which were precipitated not by the long-term forces of history but by individuals who surely deserve the epithet "heroes of evil." What is most extraordinary is that it was while Braudel was in prison, experiencing that evil personally, existentially, as he said, that he persuaded himself that such individuals and events were of little significance in history. The Holocaust as a "short-term" event—the mind boggles.

At the same time that Braudel was in that German prisoner-of-war camp producing the prototype of Annaliste history, a young American literary critic (about the same age as

Braudel) was reviewing a new edition of a much older *Annals*, that of Tacitus. Lionel Trilling was impressed by a sentence in the *Annals* which seemed to him to capture the essence of that work. "This I regard as history's highest function," Tacitus wrote, "to let no worthy action be uncommemorated, and to hold out the reprobation of posterity as a terror to evil words and deeds."[48] Trilling was not a historian, and it is unlikely that he had heard of the Annalistes, who were then little known even among professional American historians. But he was acutely aware of the history of his own times, of Nazism and Stalinism. And he was superbly alert to intellectual fashions, to the predilection, for example, of modern historians for the "long view," a view, Trilling believed, that obscured and even justified the evils of history.

> To minds of a certain sensitivity, "the long view" is the falsest historical view of all, and indeed the insistence on the length of perspective is intended precisely to overcome sensitivity—seen from a sufficient distance, it says, the corpse and hacked limbs are not so very terrible, and eventually they even begin to compose themselves into a "meaningful pattern."[49]

Trilling, like Tocqueville before him, preferred an older mode of history, a history capable, as Tacitus said, of commemorating "worthy" actions and reprobating "evil words and deeds"—a history of heroes and villains as well as ordinary people. That mode of history is inconsistent with the determinism implicit in "the long view," a view that emphasizes the kind of "general causes" Tocqueville decried as denying free will and human freedom. In one of his last public appearances, shortly before his death, Trilling described himself as "a nineteenth-century person" because he still believed in "the efficacy of the will at a time when few other intellectuals did." Asked to comment on structuralism, he recalled that thirty years earlier he had fought against Stalinism and that he would "fight structuralism today as another system antithetical to will and individual freedom."[50]

Today it is more obvious than ever that without will and freedom there can be no virtue and vice. And without virtue and vice there can be no heroes and villains. There can be only valets—valets who recognize no heroes, whether of good or of evil; indeed, who recognize no greatness of any kind: no momentous events in history, no superior works of art, literature, or philosophy, no essential distinction between the trivial and the important. If such a valet mentality prevailed, we would all, the most humble and the most eminent of us, be diminished by it. Fortunately, there is in the human spirit that which cannot long tolerate such an abasement. Having recently witnessed the overthrow of tyranny in the Soviet Union and its Eastern European satellites, we may begin to hope that our "pedagogues" will be edified and elevated by these events—great events, complete with heroes, villains, and valets.

III

From Marx to Hegel

AMONG THE MORE UNEXPECTED events of recent years—not quite as momentous as the collapse of communism but on the local scene no less startling—was the arrival of Hegel in Washington, first by courtesy of Francis Fukuyama, who introduced us to "the End of History," and then by Václav Havel, the president of the newly liberated Czechoslovakia, who informed a joint session of Congress that the lesson of recent history was that "Consciousness precedes Being." Havel didn't identify the source of that phrase, let alone explain it, but he did get a round of congressional applause when he went on to say, "and not the other way around, as the Marxists claim."[1]

"And not the other way around." His words were more telling than perhaps he knew. For they suggest not only the triumph of Hegel over Marx (mind or spirit over material existence) but also a reading of intellectual history "the other way around"—from Marx to Hegel rather than from Hegel to Marx.[2] The conventional chronological reading, from Hegel to Marx, carries with it the implication, however unintended, that Marx superseded Hegel, that he carried the history of ideas to a newer, truer, higher level—that Marx triumphed over Hegel. The reverse reading is, paradoxically, more accurate historically, for it not only affirms Hegel's belated triumph over Marx but also permits us to see more clearly what is meant by the saying "Marx stood Hegel on his head"—and what Havel meant when he said, in effect, that Hegel had been restored to his rightful upright position. The reversal is also faithful to the history of Marxism in recent years, the Hegelianization of Marxism under the guise of neo-Marxism. It is this Hegelianized Marxism that Milovan Djilas popularized under the slogan "Marxism with a human face," and that kept something of the dogma alive, at least in academic circles, long after the real Marxism had been discredited.

One of the curious things about this reversal of chronology is that we were first alerted to it by another East European, a Hungarian this time, more than half a century ago.[3] An "early" or "young" Marx was discovered—or rather, invented, which makes it even more interesting—by Georg Lukács in 1923. This was forty years after Marx's death and twenty-eight years after that of Engels. Except for Engels, none of the major Marxist (or revisionist Marxist) commentators on Marx before the Russian Revolution or in the early decades of the Revolution—Kautsky, Bernstein, Plekhanov, Lenin—had read or even knew of the works of the early Marx that now loom so large in Marxist literature: the *Economic and Philosophic Manuscripts* of 1844 and *The German*

Ideology of 1845–46. They did not know about them for the
very good reason that they had never been published, not
even in Marx's youth.*

A few years after Marx's death, Engels wrote a long review
of a book on Ludwig Feuerbach, to which he appended two
pages of an early manuscript by Marx, the now famous (at
least in Marxist circles) "Theses on Feuerbach." They were
the only pages he thought worthy of salvaging from a six-
hundred-odd-page unpublished manuscript (he did not
even mention its name, *The German Ideology*) that he and
Marx had willingly abandoned, he explained, to the "gnaw-
ings of the mice." (He meant this literally; many pages of
the manuscript had in fact been consumed by mice.) When
a Russian comrade suggested publishing Marx's early writings, Engels brusquely replied that Marx had also written
poetry as a youth, but surely no one would want to read that
now. Besides, he added, "to penetrate into that 'old story,'
one needed to have an interest in Hegel himself, which was
not the case with anybody then, or to be exact, 'neither with
Kautsky nor with Bernstein.' "[4]

After the Russian Revolution, the Marx-Engels archives
were turned over by the German Communist party to the
Communist party of the Soviet Union. In 1927, a prospectus
of the *Collected Works* of Marx and Engels was published,
including a brief abstract of Marx's early unpublished writ-

---

*A few of his other early writings had been published at the time
but were never reprinted and were almost totally unknown in his
lifetime. These include Marx's "Introduction to the Critique of
Hegel's Philosophy of Right" and "On the Jewish Question," which
were published in a German left-wing journal in Paris that survived
for all of one issue, and a lengthy polemic on Bruno and Edgar
Bauer, entitled *Holy Family*, known only to a tiny circle of German
radical émigrés.

ings. In 1932, the first volumes of that edition appeared, including some of the early writings.

The intriguing part of this story is that several years before the publication of the prospectus, Lukács, a Marxist who was also a philosopher and therefore familiar with Hegel, published a collection of essays, *History and Class Consciousness*, which made something of a stir at the time and has since become a cult book among Marxists. Lukács knew nothing of Marx's early writings, but he did know, as everyone did, that Marx had studied Hegel. And on the basis of that fact alone, reading back from Marx to Hegel, he deduced that Marx's ideas were more Hegelian in origin than anyone had suspected—that his economic concept of "exploitation," for example, derived from Hegel's metaphysical concept of "alienation." (Marx himself obscured this by contemptuously dismissing, in *The Communist Manifesto*, the idea of alienation together with all other such "philosophical nonsense.")[5]

Lukács's book, presenting this Hegelianized Marx, was published in 1923 and was promptly condemned by the Communist party of the Soviet Union as an "idealist" heresy. After Hitler came to power, Lukács (who had been living in Germany) fled to the Soviet Union, where he delivered a public recantation of his book. The irony is that by this time the early writings of Marx had been published, totally confirming Lukács's theory about the Hegelian sources of Marxism. The further irony is that throughout the thirties, at a time when Marx was becoming increasingly influential among Western intellectuals, his early writings remained virtually unknown. It was not until after the Second World War, with the revival of interest in Hegel on the part of the Frankfurt group and the Existentialists, that the young Marx began to emerge—indeed, began to overshadow the mature Marx.[6] By now this young Marx is so dominant in academic circles that one can hardly see the true features of the mature

Marx—the historic Marx, one might say, the Marx of Lenin, Stalin, and Mao.

The Hegelian system that Marx stood on its head centered on the idea of history. It is hard now, in our thoroughly historicist age, to appreciate how novel Hegel's philosophy of history was. We talk of the Kantian revolution—Kant's making of man, the knower, the center of reality, rather than the thing, the objective reality that is known. But we rarely talk of the Hegelian revolution—Hegel's making of history the center of reality.

To be sure, philosophers had always been aware of history—the transient, the ephemeral, the flux of time and change. What Hegel did was to find meaning in history—not the petty meaning that can always be found in petty events, but a grand metaphysical, teleological meaning for the whole of history. That meaning resides in what he called Reason. "The only thought which philosophy brings with it to the contemplation of history is the simple conception of *Reason*; that Reason is the sovereign of the world; that the history of the world, therefore, presents us with a rational process."[7] Earlier philosophers located reason in the nature of man or, later, in the nature of mind. Hegel located it in history, a history that thinks itself, as it were, into existence, that realizes its own rationality gradually, in one epoch after another and one people after another, until it is fully realized in a universal history that is the end of history. This Reason is not our familiar, commonsense, everyday reason, the reason we bring to the ordinary events of our lives. It is, so to speak, a capitalized Reason (in German, of course, all nouns are capitalized), a cosmic Reason, a Reason that makes history meaningful—meaningful not in the sense that it makes history fully comprehensible to human beings, but that it makes history meaningful and rational in and of itself.

This is not to say that Hegel believed that everything that happens in history is rational—although this is the charge commonly brought against him. The idea that everything that is, is rational, therefore legitimate, would seem to legitimize the whole of the existing order, the status quo. "The real world," he is quoted as saying, "is as it ought to be." The rest of the sentence is rarely quoted: ". . . that the truly good—the universal divine reason—is not a mere abstraction, but a vital principle capable of realizing itself."[8] "*Capable* of realizing itself"—not already real. At any moment it is "as it ought to be," but that "ought to be" is itself constantly changing. Thus, Reason is only partially realized and the real is only partially rational. If Reason were already fully realized, then history would be at an end, and we would truly be in that state we have heard so much about lately, the End of History.

It is by means of the dialectic of history, the dynamic of history, that the rational gradually realizes itself in history. This dialectic depends upon the double meaning of "history": empirical, factual, actual history—the "panorama" of history, as Hegel puts it (lowercase history, we might say); and History as it is penetrated by Reason, rational History (uppercase History). Hegel does not deny the reality of actual history, as some have claimed. On the contrary, he insists upon it, for it is only through actual history that rational History emerges.

Actual history, history as experienced by human beings in their daily lives, is full of "*un*reason"—violence, evil, vice, decay.[9] It is here that men act out their needs, passions, interests, characters, and talents. And it is by this means, by individuals seeking the satisfaction of their particular wants—not by divine intervention or preordained providence—that Reason emerges. This is the "cunning of Reason"—Reason using passion and interest to achieve its ends, using the particular to realize the universal. In pursuing their own passions and interests, individuals unwittingly produce results beyond their purposes. "They gratify their own interest; but something further is thereby accomplished, latent in the actions in question, though not present to their consciousness, and not included in their design."[10]

Some people, "world-historical individuals," further the course of history and accelerate the emergence of Reason more directly and dramatically. But even they are only the unwitting instruments of Reason. They bring History to a new stage of development without knowing what they are doing. They think they are acting in their own interests or in accord with their own ideas and ideals, but they contain within themselves an unconscious inner spirit that germinates within them and finally bursts forth, like a kernel from a shell, a seed from "the womb of time." It was thus that Caesar, seeking only to promote his own autocratic power, fulfilled the historical destiny of Rome and the world.[11]

As Reason unfolds in History, so does the Idea or Spirit immanent in History—the consciousness of Freedom. Here we come upon another common misreading of Hegel. One of his editors sums up Hegel's thesis about the evolution of Freedom: "In past Oriental civilizations *one* was free; in classical antiquity, Greece and Rome, *some* were free; and in modern Germanic and Anglo-Saxon civilizations, *all* are free."[12] In fact, what Hegel says is:

> The Orientals have not attained the knowledge that Spirit—Man *as such*—is free; and because they do not know this, they are not free. They only know that *one* [man] *is free*. But on this very account, the freedom of that one is only caprice. . . . The consciousness of Freedom first arose among the Greeks, and therefore

they were free; but they, and the Romans likewise, knew only that *some* are free—not man as such. Even Plato and Aristotle did not know this. The Greeks, therefore, had slaves; . . . a fact, moreover, which made that liberty on the one hand only an accidental, transient and limited growth; on the other hand, constituted it a rigorous thraldom of our common nature—of the Human. The German nations, under the influence of Christianity, were the first to attain the consciousness, that man, as man, is free: that it is the *freedom* of Spirit which constitutes its essence.[13]

Hegel is talking not about the evolution of Freedom but about the evolution of the *consciousness* of Freedom. He does not say that in Oriental civilizations only one person was free, in classical antiquity some people were free, and in modernity all are free—but rather that in Oriental civilizations men only "know" that one is free; in antiquity they "knew" that some were free; and in Western modernity they attained the "consciousness" that man as man is free. Consciousness is paramount in Freedom, just as Reason is paramount in History. And it is the consciousness of Freedom that is the unfolding agenda of History. And so, too, as Havel reminds us, "Consciousness precedes Being." For Hegel, Consciousness is the primary, determining condition of our Being, our existence—unlike Marx, for whom Being, material existence, preceded and determined Consciousness.

Which brings us to Marx—or, rather, to his predecessors, the Young Hegelians. For it was they, not Marx, who first stood Hegel on his head. Hegel was, in a sense, a victim of his own dialectic: his thesis was confronted with its antithesis, in the form of Young Hegelianism, out of which emerged a new synthesis, Marxism. What is so fascinating about this story is how rapidly this movement of ideas worked itself out. Trotsky used to warn those deviating from the party line: If you say A you have to say B, if B then C, and so on until you reach Z—that is, if you start with revisionism, you will end up in counter-revolution. And so it was with the Young Hegelians. Each deviation inspired a greater deviation, until the entire, beautifully articulated structure of Hegelianism lay in ruins.

Hegel died in 1831, leaving behind two rival groups of Young Hegelians, the Left and the Right. The traditional distinction between the two is that the Right accepted the *content* of Hegel's thought—Reason in History, and the modern state as the embodiment of Reason; while the Left accepted the *form*—the dialectic as the agent or motive power of change. A more compelling difference at the time concerned religion. The Right interpreted Hegel's Reason as equivalent to God and thus his philosophy as a rational support of Christianity; while the Left took his Reason as a repudiation of Christianity, as the replacement of religion and revelation by philosophy and reason.

It was, in fact, religion that preoccupied the Young Hegelians, the Left as well as the Right.* The controversy started in 1835, only four years after Hegel's death, with the publica-

---

*Seeing Marxism as a purely secular phenomenon, many commentators have either denied or belittled the role that religion played in its development. Sidney Hook, in his influential book *From Hegel to Marx* (1950), interprets the quarrel between Right and Left Hegelians as political, with religion only the pretext of the argument. This interpretation originated with Engels in his book on Feuerbach (1888), where he claimed that the religious issue was a mask for political differences to avoid censorship. In fact, the religious censorship was as severe as the political. The philosopher Johann Fichte, for example, was forced out of his professorship at Jena on the charge of atheism.

tion of David Strauss's *Life of Jesus.* The book burst like a bomb-
shell throughout literate Europe, although in retrospect it
may seem mild enough. Its thesis is deceptively simple: The
miracles recounted in the Gospels, including the divinity of
Christ, are not literally true, but they are mythically true.
They express the mythmaking consciousness of the early
Christians; they are the primitive communal beliefs that gave
meaning, and Reason, to the experiences of that community.

A few years later, Bruno Bauer took the argument a large
step forward by denying not only the miracles and divinity
of Christ, but also the mythical and communal nature of
Christian beliefs. The Gospels, he claimed, are nothing more
than the creations of individual men expressing their private
beliefs. To ascribe to them any mythical or communal meaning is to be insufficiently rational and critical (that is, philosophical).

Both Strauss and Bauer thought of themselves as Hegelians, each insisting that his interpretation was the truly
Hegelian one. Feuerbach was the first of the Young Hegelians to break with Hegel. In *Essence of Christianity*, religion is
said to represent not only a failure of man's consciousness,
of his critical reason, but also a failure of man's humanity,
of his ability to realize himself fully as a man. Hegel's
Reason is the "last rational support of theology," because it
makes of Reason a God, an idea or spirit outside of man. To
return God to man, one has to "turn Hegel upside down."
It is not God who created man in God's image, but man
who created God in man's image. So long as man retains the
idea of God—or Reason, or any cosmic purpose outside
of and superior to himself—man will be alienated from
his own true being. He can overcome that alienation by
emancipating himself not only from Christianity but also
from Hegel's Reason. The "essence" of man is man himself;
man's only religion is the "Religion of Humanity." *"Homo
homini deus est"*—"Man is the God of man."[14]

Only three years after Feuerbach turned Hegel upside down, another Young Hegelian, Max Stirner (né Johann Kaspar Schmidt), turned Feuerbach upside down. Stirner's *The Ego and His Own* is a thoroughgoing denial of any transcendent philosophic principle, of Feuerbach's man-as-God as much as of Hegel's Reason-as-God. The Religion of Humanity, he said, is still a religion.* The only reality is the "Ego," the "Self," the "I," the "unique one." Beyond that there is nothing—no religion, no morality, no community, no meaning, no truth. Long before Nietzsche, Stirner wrote, "As long as you believe in the truth, you do not believe in yourself, and you are a—*servant*, a—*religious man*."[15] *The Ego and His Own* concludes:

> I am *owner* of my might, and I am so when I know myself as *unique*. In the *unique one* the owner himself returns into his creative nothing, of which he is born. Every higher essence above me, be it God, be it man, weakens the feeling of my uniqueness, and pales only before the sun of this consciousness. If I found my affair on myself, the unique one, then my concern rests on its transitory, mortal creator, who consumes himself, and I may say:
> I have founded my affair on nothing.[16]

This was the culmination of Young Hegelianism, a nihilism that was the antithesis of Hegel's rationalism. And this movement of thought—from Hegelianism to Nietzschean-

---

*Stirner proved to be right. Today, Feuerbach is part of the literature of theology. A recent paperback edition of *Essence of Christianity* contains a foreword by Reinhold Niebuhr and an introduction by Karl Barth. It is also interesting that the translation of this edition is by George Eliot.

ism, one might say*—took place in a single decade and on the part of a very small group of very bright, very bold, very articulate, and very young men. (Strauss was all of twenty-seven when his book took Europe by storm, and the others were about his age.)

In a sense, Hegel was responsible for it all. In retrospect, one can see that his thesis was bound to produce its antithesis. His idea of Reason was so absolute, so intoxicating, that his followers were inevitably tempted to the messianic aspiration of actualizing Reason—not at the end of history but in the present. By the same token, the Freedom that Hegel saw as unfolding gradually in History, this too the Young Hegelians tried to realize, in its totality, here and now. Stirner went still further, denying Reason and putting in its place a radically individualistic—indeed, nihilistic—freedom, divorced from any ideal of humanity itself. But it was Hegel, one might say, who was the real revolutionary. By creating a God of Reason rather than revelation, he inspired others (like Feuerbach) to create a man-god, and still others (like Stirner), a godless man.

It was at this point, and in this milieu, that Marx appeared on the scene. As intellectual generations are counted (ten or fifteen years to the generation), Marx and Engels were a generation younger than the other Young Hegelians. For a brief period they were associated with some of the lesser-known Young Hegelians (Moses Hess, Arnold Ruge), and their earliest writings were much indebted to them. In 1845, when Marx was twenty-seven (exactly Strauss's age when he

---

*There was a revival of interest in Stirner in the 1890s, concurrently with Nietzscheanism. *The Ego and His Own* was republished then for the first time.

launched his heresy upon the world), he and Engels started to write *The German Ideology*, a diatribe against Bauer, Feuerbach, and Stirner. One can see why the book was never published. It was an exceedingly long, vituperative, often scatological attack on the Young Hegelians, accusing them, among other things, of being mired in the dunghill of religion because they were all obsessed with consciousness and self-consciousness rather than with the real world of material conditions (thus the religious epithets used to mock them—"the blessed Max" for Stirner, "Saint Bruno" for Bauer).

The Communist Manifesto, written three years later, was Marx's alternative to both Hegelianism and Young Hegelianism. (This too was a joint production of Marx and Engels; if it is generally attributed to Marx, it is because of his later preeminence as well as for the sake of convenience.) The *Manifesto*, even more than *Capital*, reveals the essence of Marxism. It also reveals Marx's dexterity in standing Hegel on his head, even while appropriating one of Hegel's crucial ideas, the idea of History.

The first striking fact about the *Manifesto* is that it is not so much a manifesto, a call to action, as it is a history or, more precisely, a philosophy of history—indeed, a contra-Hegel *Philosophy of History*. In place of Reason as the moving force of History, there is the class struggle: "The history of all hitherto existing society is the history of class struggles."[17] And in place of the Hegelian epochs of history defined by the consciousness of freedom, the Marxist epochs are defined by the mode of production and class relations.

History is as crucial to Marx's schema as to Hegel's. For Marx, as for Hegel, history has its own inexorable, teleological necessity; the movement of history may be temporarily deflected, but it cannot be permanently stayed. The driving force of history, however, is radically different. Where Hegel's History is driven by a cosmic Reason and the spirit of Freedom, Marx's is driven by material production and the class struggle. Where Hegel has the kernel of Spirit bursting through the shell of actuality to bring History to a new stage of rational development, Marx, using an almost identical metaphor, sees class relations and productive forces "burst asunder" by their inner contradictions, thus generating the revolution that brings history to a new stage of social development.[18] Where Hegel relies upon the "cunning of Reason" to further the progress of History—History operating through the passions and interests of individuals—Marx relies upon what might be called the "cunning of matter"—History progressing by means of the contradictions in the material mode of production and the relations of classes.

Unlike Hegel, Marx has no heroes, no "world-historical individuals," to hasten the movement of history. He has no individuals at all in his schema. Instead he has classes, and above all he has the "world-historical" proletariat.[19] This raises an interesting question: Why did Marx, addressing himself to the proletariat, speaking on its behalf and in its name, present it in so unattractive a light? The word itself is pejorative; deriving from *proles*, meaning "offspring," it originally referred to the lowest class of Roman citizen, who served the state only by producing children. The account of the proletariat in the *Manifesto* is no less unflattering. The proletariat is depicted as not only poor but getting poorer every day, working longer hours for less wages, sinking deeper and deeper into pauperism and slavery, barely able to "prolong and reproduce a bare existence"—indeed, barely human at all, having become little more than a "commodity," an "appendage of the machine."[20]

The proletariat is thus dehumanized, lacking all the moral and social qualities normally attributed to human beings: a sense of law, morality, nationality, religion, culture, family, freedom. All these, Marx says, are purely "bourgeois preju-

dices," "bourgeois notions."[21] On the subject of family, he is
especially brutal. The bourgeois family is based "on capital,
on private gain"; the proletariat, having no capital, has no
family. Communists do not have to introduce a "community
of women" since "it has existed almost from time immemo-
rial." The bourgeoisie, when they are not seeking out prostitutes and seducing one another's wives, have "the wives and
daughters of their proletarians at their disposal." Finally,
most brutally, "all family ties among the proletarians are
torn asunder, and their children transformed into simple
articles of commerce and instruments of labor."[22]*

This is an extraordinary picture of the class that was to be
the bearer, the hero, of the revolution. Later Marxists called

---

*Engels had drawn much the same picture of the English proletar-
iat a few years earlier. Having lived in England for less than two
years, he felt qualified not only to predict an imminent revolution
in England but also to analyze the "condition of the working class"
("class" in the singular, contrary to English usage but in accord
with Marxist theory). That class included tens of thousands of
homeless wandering the streets and millions more crowded in the
foulest slums, clothed in rags, sickly, crippled, stunted, deformed,
dying of starvation or existing in a state of near-starvation. Its
moral condition was equally appalling, for it was reduced to a state
of utter degradation, more bestial than human, given to drink,
violence, crime, and licentiousness—"a race wholly apart" from
the bourgeoisie. Here too the family was practically nonexistent,
destroyed by the factories and by filthy, crowded homes lacking
any domestic comfort. When it was not "wholly dissolved," it was
"turned upside down," with the wife working and the unemployed
husband at home, a situation that "unsexes the man and takes from
the woman all womanliness." In addition to the sexual promiscuity
that was rife among the workers themselves, the women were at
the mercy of their employers, who enjoyed the traditional privilege
of the master over the slave, the *jus primae noctis*—except that the
employer could exercise that right at any time.[23]

it the "immiseration" thesis—the idea that things are terrible and can only get worse until the cataclysm occurs that will make everything not only better but perfect. But this abstraction does not do justice to the portrait. The question is: Why did Marx and Engels depict the proletariat in this brutal fashion, not so much as a class apart as a species apart? It was not only tactless, to say the least; they were, after all, addressing that class and calling on it to wage the revolution. Their portrait was demonstrably untrue. It had never been true; things had never been that bad. Certainly by 1848, when the *Manifesto* was written, it was less true than ever, for by then the conditions of the working classes were clearly improving—economically, politically, socially, morally. And it became less true as the century went on, although Marxists continued to hold to that "immiseration" theory.

It was not true, but it was necessary for Marx's purpose. It was necessary in order to create a historical schema that was thoroughly deterministic. Only if the proletariat was reduced to its lowest level, to the point of total pauperization and dehumanization, would the revolution be a historical necessity—not a matter of will, or desire, or consciousness, but of literal, physical necessity. Only at this stage of history, when the crisis of the proletariat was at its height, when the workers could barely sustain and reproduce themselves, when they had nothing to lose but their chains—and when simultaneously the crisis of capitalism, brought about by the contradictions of the capitalist mode of production, was at its height—only then is communism inevitable, because it is then a product of the "real movement" of history. Communism is not "an *ideal* to which reality will have to adjust itself." It is the reality itself—the reality of a proletariat that exists "world-historically," and of a communism that has a "world-historical existence."²⁴ And it is the depiction of this reality, of the real movement of history, that makes his philosophy, Marx claimed, not "speculation" but "real, positive science"—indeed, that makes it not a philosophy at all, for "when reality is depicted, philosophy as an independent branch of activity loses its medium of existence."[25]

It was Engels who coined the term "Historical Materialism" to describe Marxism. Some commentators maintain that the concept was peculiar to Engels, that Marx would not have used or approved of it. In fact, it precisely describes what Marx did when he stood Hegel on his head. He retained the crucial idea of history that made communism inevitable and "scientific"—he even retained some of Hegel's distinctive terms (such as "world-historical")—while giving history an entirely different motivating force. If Hegelianism can be characterized as "Historical Idealism" (which is not a bad label for it), Marxism can properly be described as "Historical Materialism."

In rejecting Hegel's Idealism, Marx rejected not only Reason but also Freedom as the impelling force of history. This is another extraordinary feature of the *Manifesto*—the conspicuous absence of the appeal to Freedom. One might think that Marx would have invoked that idea, if only for rhetorical effect. He could have condemned capitalism for depriving the proletariat of freedom—the freedom to speak, act, believe (or disbelieve), organize, vote. And he could have made it one of the arguments in favor of communism that it would give the proletariat the freedom enjoyed only by the bourgeoisie. It is a tribute to Marx's honesty and rigor that he did not do this. On the contrary, he spurned the idea of freedom.

Every reference to freedom in the *Manifesto* (with a single exception) is invidious. "Your bourgeois notions of freedom, culture, law, etc., . . . are but the outgrowth of the conditions of bourgeois production and bourgeois property."[26] Communists are accused of wanting to abolish not only property but also individuality and freedom—"and rightly so," Marx concedes. "The abolition of bourgeois individuality, bourgeois independence, and bourgeois freedom is undoubtedly aimed at," for bourgeois freedom means nothing more than "free trade, free selling and buying."[27] The ideas of religious liberty and freedom of consciousness which arose in the eighteenth century "merely gave expression to the sway of free competition within the domain of knowledge." They are no more "eternal truths" than are the ideas of "Freedom, Justice, etc."; all of these are part of "the social consciousness of past ages." These ideas, too, Communists are accused of wanting to abolish—and again, Marx implies, rightly so, for "the Communist revolution is the most radical rupture with traditional property relations; no wonder that its development involves the most radical rupture with traditional ideas."[28]

The one exception, the only positive reference to freedom in the whole of the *Manifesto*, appears in the very last sentence, in the description of communism: "In place of the old bourgeois society, with its classes and class antagonisms, we shall have an association in which the free development of each is the condition for the free development of all."[29] Period. End of quotation, end of description. "Free development"—what did Marx mean by that? The only clue we have is in *The German Ideology*. It is there that Marx gives us a memorable image of communist society enjoying a freedom totally unlike anything that had previously gone under the name of freedom. In contrast to bourgeois society, where each person is confined to a particular productive role, a communist society "regulates the general production and thus makes it possible for me to do one thing today and another tomorrow, to hunt in the morning, fish in the afternoon, rear cattle in the evening, criticize [philosophize] after dinner, just as I have a mind, without ever becoming hunter, fisherman, shepherd, or critic."[30]

A more prosaic mind may find it difficult to conceive of a communist society that can "regulate" production and at the same time leave everyone free to do as he likes every minute of the day. But then, it is also difficult to conceive of *any* society where everyone is quite so free to do whatever he likes whenever he likes. Can one really "rear cattle" (milk cows) only in the evening? And what of raising crops, which is curiously omitted here? Or producing industrial goods, which also does not appear? Does Marx suppose that communism will do away with industrialism (which is, after all, based upon a division of labor and thus the organization of labor) together with capitalism? One wonders what the proletariat of Marx's day, who were not hunters, fishers, cattle rearers, or philosophers, but rather agricultural laborers and factory workers, would have made of this vision of freedom. It is understandable that Marx should have chosen not to dwell on it—indeed, why he said so little, in the *Manifesto* and elsewhere, about the final stage of communism.

If freedom in the conventional, "bourgeois" sense had no meaning or value for Marx (except as a strategy in the struggle against capitalism), neither did "consciousness." This too is puzzling at first sight. Why was Marx so insistent upon the principle "Life is not determined by consciousness, but consciousness by life"?[31] Why was he so determined to relegate consciousness—ideas, beliefs, values, culture—to the "superstructure" of reality? Why did he equate "intellectual products" with "material products," so that the abolition of bourgeois property necessarily entailed the abolition of the "class culture"?[32] Why did he deprive communism of the powerful support of such "bourgeois" ideas as liberty, equality, fraternity, justice, natural rights?

In fact, this materialistic theory of consciousness created serious problems for Marx and Engels, who were both indubitably products of bourgeois culture and society. (Engels was in fact a certified capitalist, a part-owner of several factories; this is where he got the money to support Marx.) How could they have developed a consciousness—ideas, principles, values—so inimical to their own class interests? How, indeed, could they have created Marxism? And how could they have attracted so many disciples who were also bourgeois and who were acting against their material interests?

These, however, were minor inconveniences compared with the advantages of a rigorous materialism and determinism. And that materialism and determinism precluded both freedom and consciousness. Those were ideological remnants of the past. It was the future Marx was interested in— a future not dependent on the vagaries of men's ideas or on their conscious choices and actions.

Marxism did not win converts because of its economic theories about value or surplus value; the economists soon exposed the weaknesses of those theories. Nor did it win converts because of its predictions about the pauperization of the proletariat and the proletarianization of the petite bourgeoisie; the economy itself soon belied those predictions. Nor did it win converts because of its insistence on the class struggle and revolution; a school of Marxist revisionism soon exposed the futility of that strategy. Nor did it win converts because it was full of compassion for human suffering; Marx himself had nothing but contempt for those who were interested in the proletariat merely, as he said in the *Manifesto*, as the "suffering class."*

---

*This was one of Marx's complaints against the Utopian Socialists. Instead of seeing the proletariat in their historical role as the bearer of the class struggle, the Utopians were "conscious of caring" for

Marxism won converts because it promised to conquer the future. And it expected to do so because of the potent combination of materialism and historicism. The success of Marxism was to be assured by the real movement of history—not by individuals pursuing their ideas and ideals, but by a class that necessarily, inexorably, even unwittingly, would bring about the revolution that would carry history into its next, and final, stage of development.

Nothing is as seductive as the assurance of success. It is sometimes said that the weakness of Marxism was its historical determinism. Why fight for communism if its success was assured? Why form or join a Communist party if the proletariat itself, by its very existence, would bring about the revolution?* But these are the arguments of logicians. Politicians know that the bandwagon is the most effective political vehicle. What Marx called the real movement of history, we know as the "tide of history," the "wave of the future." Communism, the classless society, makes its appearance, however vaguely, only at the end of history, but the movement toward it is in the present. And it is the promise of that utopian end, unspecified and undescribed, that justifies the harsh necessities of the present—the bloodshed and strife inherent in the class struggle and revolution, the tyr-

---

them as "the most suffering class." "Only from the point of view of being the most suffering class does the proletariat exist for them."[33]

*In the *Manifesto*, Marx feebly addressed this last question by saying that the Communist party has no "interests" and no "sectarian principles" apart from those of the proletariat; it is merely the "most advanced and resolute" of the working-class parties, with a clearer "understanding [of] the line of march."[34] Later, Lenin gave the Communist party a much more prominent and positive role, both theoretically and practically; the dictatorship of the proletariat was in fact the dictatorship of the party.

anny and injustice inevitable in that intermediate stage of socialism known as the dictatorship of the proletariat.

To win the future, Marx was prepared to forfeit man—to "abolish man" (as C. S. Lewis put it). Hannah Arendt has said that no thinker ever reduced man to an *animal laborans* as totally as Marx did. Locke, she points out, made of labor the source of all property; Adam Smith made of labor the source of all wealth; Marx made of labor the very essence of man.[35] One might add that the very word "proletariat"— in place of the terms familiar at the time, "workers" and "working classes"—is mechanistic. "Workers" are individuals, and "working classes" testifies to the plurality and heterogeneity of those classes. Moreover, both preserve the dignity associated with "work." "Proletariat," on the other hand, denies the individuality and variety of workers, recognizing only a single, undifferentiated class—a class that does not share a common ("generic," as the Marxist says) human nature with other classes but is totally distinctive and identified entirely as an instrument of production. Marx accused the bourgeoisie of reducing the proletariat to a "commodity," an "appendage" of the machine.[36] But he himself did just that.*

---

*In his Young Hegelian days, Marx spoke of the proletariat in very different terms: as a class that is "not a class"; an estate that represents the "dissolution of all estates"; a sphere that has a "universal" character because it represents "universal suffering"; that claims "no particular right" because "no particular wrong but wrong generally" is perpetrated against it; that invokes no "historical" but only a "human title"; that can "emancipate" itself only by emancipating all of society; that "can win itself only through the *complete re-winning of man.*"[37] This was written in 1844, and it is the last time Marx spoke in this "humanistic" fashion. The next year, following the publication of Stirner's book, he bitterly condemned this conception of the proletariat and of man. And in the *Manifesto*

The Marxist combination of materialism and determinism is fatally anti-humanistic. It denies a consciousness, a mind, that is independent of material conditions and class relations. It denies a will and volition that are capable of shaping the course of history. It denies an individuality that is not reducible to class. It denies both the idea and the reality of freedom, a freedom that is something more than the "bourgeois" freedom to buy and sell. It denies a morality that transcends class interests. And it denies the spirituality of man—in either the orthodox religious sense, or the philosophical Hegelian sense, or the humanistic Feuerbachian sense.

By putting Marxism back into the Hegelian context, one can see what it meant to stand Hegel on his head. Paraphrasing the memorable saying of Freud's, "Where the Id was, there the Ego shall be," one may say of Marx: "Where Spirit was, there Matter shall be." The so-called "humanistic" Marx, celebrated by neo-Marxists, is an oxymoron. It is, in fact, an insult to Marx, for it belies everything he sought so hard to achieve. As Yogi Berra might have said, "If Marx were alive today, he'd be turning in his grave."

Marx would also be turning in his grave as he contemplated the events of recent years—the repudiation not only of the Communist regimes in Russia and Eastern Europe but also of the ideology of Marxism. He would have been even more distressed by the thought that his defeat was, in a sense, Hegel's triumph. Intellectuals who once read Marx are now reading Hegel—and interpreting and reinterpreting him quite as they once did Marx. And even the proletariat (or people—"proletariat" being as obsolete as Marxism), in rejecting communism, was affirming something like Hegel's Reason, Freedom, Spirit, Consciousness.

---

he derided the "German, or 'True,' Socialism" that still held to this idea.

Perestroika may have triggered the revolution (or counter-revolution, Marx might have said), but glasnost carried it far beyond the intentions of its initiator. The kernel in the shell that finally burst forth, the seed in the womb of time, was the spirit of freedom, a spirit that almost three-quarters of a century of communism could not eradicate.

Havel was quite right. If the freedom he fought for was not quite Hegel's Freedom, it had far more in common with Hegel than with Marx. And the lesson he learned from that struggle, that "Consciousness precedes Being, and not the other way around," was, however obscure to his congressional audience, pure Hegel. There is much else in Hegel that Havel, no doubt, deplores, as do many conservatives as well as liberals. But on that key issue, the primacy of Consciousness and its correlates—Reason, Spirit, Freedom—we can all learn from Havel, as he did from Hegel. The "real movement" of history, it turns out, is fueled not by matter but by spirit, by the will to freedom.

IV

Liberty: "One Very Simple Principle"?

THE END OF THE Cold War has liberated us in
more ways than we might have thought, liberated us from
the tyranny of communism and the shackles of Marxism,
and liberated us as well to reexamine the liberalism that is
now triumphant. For more than half a century, confronted
with the double threat of Nazism and communism, the urgent problem facing us was: How can liberalism defend itself
against totalitarianism? How can a society that is individualistic, pluralistic, pacific, devoted to private pleasures and
domestic tranquillity, prevail against an enemy that is collec-
tivist, authoritarian, militaristic, mobilized for power and
conquest? The defeat of Nazism and the collapse of the
Soviet empire have conclusively proved that totalitarianism
is not only oppressive and murderous; it is inefficient and
fatally vulnerable.

Now we must confront another problem: not how liberalism can defend itself against totalitarianism, but how it can defend itself against itself—against its own weaknesses and excesses. In the Marxist jargon that has survived the death of the Marxist regimes, this is the new "problematic" of liberalism. How can a society that celebrates the virtues of liberty, individuality, variety, and tolerance sustain itself when those virtues, carried to extremes, threaten to subvert that liberal society and, with it, those very virtues?

The problem is not political but social, cultural, and moral; it is the ethos of liberalism that is at issue. Nor is it a new problem, for it goes back at least to the "classical liberalism," as we now call it, of the nineteenth century. The question of its genealogy is of more than academic interest. If the problem is inherent in classical liberalism, then it is not, as we might otherwise think, an aberration, peculiar to American democracy (American "exceptionalism"), or to "consumerist" capitalism, or to "post-industrial" society. These circumstances may exacerbate it, but they did not create it. And if this is so, then it is a matter of concern for all countries, the newly liberated as well as those with long-established liberal traditions.

The classic text of classical liberalism is, of course, John Stuart Mill's *On Liberty*. It is also, by now, the classic text of a libertarian conservatism that regards itself as the true heir of classical liberalism. It is also the classic text of radicalism, at least of the particular school of radicalism that sees itself as carrying out the failed agenda of liberalism, the goal of true liberation. It is, in short, something of an icon of modernity, giving intellectual authority and legitimacy to ideas and attitudes that dominate our society.

It also has the virtue of posing the issue in terms that are even more relevant today than they were in Mill's time. The first page of *On Liberty* informs us that the problem of liberty is no longer the problem of political liberty, of the struggle against a tyrannical regime imposing its arbitrary will on an oppressed populace. That problem, Mill assures us, has been solved by the establishment of popular government—at least in the more advanced countries, and potentially in all others as they reach the level of a mature civilization.[1] The problem now facing liberty is a new form of tyranny, a "social tyranny" exercised by the populace itself over the individual.

The opening sentence of *On Liberty* announces its subject, "Civil, or Social Liberty," and defines its province: "the nature and limits of the power which can be legitimately exercised by society over the individual."[2] The magnitude of the subject makes even more dramatic the "one very simple principle" that is at the heart of it.[3] The passage describing this principle must be read in its entirety to appreciate how simple and also how absolute it is:

> The object of this Essay is to assert one very simple principle, as entitled to govern absolutely the dealings of society with the individual in the way of compulsion and control, whether the means used be physical force in the form of legal penalties, or the moral coercion of public opinion. That principle is, that the sole end for which mankind are warranted, individually or collectively, in interfering with the liberty of action of any of their number, is self-protection. That the only purpose for which power can be rightfully exercised over any member of a civilised community, against his will, is to prevent harm to others. His own good, either physical or moral, is not a sufficient warrant. He cannot rightfully be compelled to do or forbear because it will be better for him to do so, because it will make him happier, because, in the opinions of others, to do so would be wise, or even right. These are good reasons for remonstrating with him, or persuading him, or entreating him, but not for compelling him, or visiting him with any evil in case he do otherwise. To justify that, the

conduct from which it is desired to deter him must be calculated to produce evil to someone else. The only part of the conduct of any one, for which he is amenable to society, is that which concerns others. In the part which merely concerns himself, his independence is, of right, absolute. Over himself, over his own body and mind, the individual is sovereign.[4]

The rhetoric is as simple and absolute as the principle itself. "One very simple principle" governs "absolutely" the relations of the individual and society; the "sole" end for which society may interfere with the liberty of an individual is self-protection; the "only" purpose for which power can be exercised over an individual is to prevent harm to others; the "only" part of the individual's conduct amenable to society is that which concerns others; in the part that concerns himself his independence is "absolute"; over his "own" body and mind he is "sovereign."*

The rhetoric also points to a radical disjunction between the individual and society—indeed, an adversarial relation-

---

*The paragraph following this seems to introduce further qualifications, but they are so minimal as to be of little practical effect. The principle is said to apply "only to human beings in the maturity of their faculties," and not to "those backward states of society in which the race itself may be considered as in its nonage." But Mill defines maturity literally to exclude only "children, or young persons below the age which the law may fix as that of manhood or womanhood"; and the requisite stage of civilization, he says, has "long since [been] reached in all nations with whom we need here concern ourselves."[5] There is nothing in these qualifications to warrant the view of some commentators that Mill meant to limit the principle of liberty to those individuals of superior intellectual or moral competence, or to an exalted level of civilization—still less that it was meant to apply only to "a mature public carrying on its discussion in a restrained and civilized way."[6]

ship, with the individual assigned all the positive, honorific attributes, and society the negative, pejorative ones. Thus the individual is endowed with "liberty" and "will"; his own "good" is entirely his own concern; his "independence" is absolute; he is "sovereign." Society, on the other hand, acts by way of "compulsion," "control," "force," "coercion," "interference," "tyranny." These negative qualities apply to society whether it is acting by means of "physical force in the form of legal penalties" or by the "moral coercion of public opinion." Even in the one circumstance where society can rightfully "interfere," its purpose is negative, to prevent "harm" or "evil" to others. It is explicitly enjoined from doing anything positive or desirable, from trying to further the individual's "good," or to make him "better" or "happier," or to do what it might think "wise" or "right."

This "one very simple principle," Mill goes on to say, governs the realms of thought and speech, of action ("individuality"), and of combination (unions of individuals). And it is this principle, not the political system, that determines whether a country is free. "No society in which these liberties are not, on the whole, respected, is free, whatever may be its form of government; and none is completely free in which they do not exist absolute and unqualified."[7]

As liberty of thought is absolute, so is liberty of speech, which is "inseparable" from the liberty of thought. Liberty of speech, moreover, is essential not only for its own sake but for the sake of truth, which requires absolute liberty for the utterance of unpopular and even demonstrably false opinions. Indeed, false or unpopular opinions are so important to truth that they should be encouraged and disseminated by "devil's advocates" if necessary, for only by the "collision of adverse opinions" can the most certain of truths survive as live truth rather than "dead dogma."[8]

Liberty of action—"individuality," as it is called in *On Liberty*—is only one degree less absolute than that of thought and speech, for it is subject to the qualification of harm to others. Apart from that, it is inviolable because individuality is an absolute good in itself. Again, the rhetoric is revealing, individuality being associated with such positive words as "independence," "originality," "spontaneity," "genius," "variety," "diversity," "experiment," "choice," "vigor," "development," "desire," "feeling"; and the threat to individuality with such negative words as "conformity," "mediocrity," "restraint," the "yoke" of opinion, the "tyranny" of society, the "despotism" of custom. Some words that in normal usage are at best equivocal—"impulse," "peculiarity," "eccentricity"— have entirely favorable connotations as attributes of individuality; while others—"law," "tradition," "custom," "opinion," "discipline," "obedience"—are unmistakably negative because they appear to restrict individuality.*

Just as the freedom of discussion is deemed good in itself, even when it results in the freedom of error, so individuality is good in itself even when an individual's "plan of life" or "experiments of living" are not notably good, or may even be bad. In an earlier age, Mill explains, there was no advan-

---

*One obvious negative term, "license," appears nowhere in the book, perhaps because it suggests that there can be an excess of liberty. Some commentators assume that Mill meant to distinguish between liberty and license.[9] Yet if he meant to do so, it is difficult to see why he did not do so explicitly. "License" was a common word in his time, as it had been for centuries. Milton makes play with the word: "But lest I should be condemned of introducing licence, while I oppose licencing . . ." Locke describes the state of nature: "Though this be a state of liberty, yet it is not a state of licence." And Montesquieu says that when a "spirit of extreme equality" exists among the citizenry, "virtue can no longer subsist in the republic. . . . Licence will soon become general."[10]

tage in individuals acting differently from the mass, "unless they acted not only differently but better." Today, however, the "mere example of non-conformity" or "eccentricity" is itself a virtue. And it is a virtue not only for "persons of genius" but for the "average man," who should be encouraged to defy custom and cultivate his individual mode of life, "not because it is the best in itself, but because it is his own mode."[11]

This is the barest skeleton of Mill's extraordinary essay, but it is enough to suggest just how extraordinary it is. No discussion of *On Liberty* is complete without a tribute to its noble precursor, John Milton's *Areopagitica*. Yet Mill does not mention that work in his essay, perhaps for the good reason that Milton's idea of liberty is not at all his own. Milton passionately defended freedom of the press; his tract was provoked by a parliamentary law requiring the licensing of printed works. But his argument did not extend to freedom of action. And even freedom of the press was restricted to a degree that Mill would have found intolerable, for it did not tolerate "popery, and open superstition," nor that which is "impious or evil absolutely either against faith or manners."[12]

Nor does Mill cite as predecessors any of the other thinkers who might be expected to appear in a discussion of liberty: Spinoza, Locke, Montesquieu, Kant, Paine, Jefferson, Macaulay, Tocqueville—again, for good reason.* No

---

*Locke, Kant, and Tocqueville are mentioned in passing but not in connection with liberty. The omission of Tocqueville is most conspicuous, since Mill was clearly indebted to him for the idea of "social tyranny" and the "tyranny of the majority." (The quotation marks around the latter expression in *On Liberty* are an implicit tribute to Tocqueville.)[13]

one of them went so far as to propose anything like an absolute, or near-absolute, principle of liberty. Each limited or qualified liberty in a significant respect: liberty of speech, "but not out of anger, hatred, or a desire to introduce any change in the state on his own authority" (Spinoza)[14]; liberty, but only within the law and not for "opinions contrary to human society, or to those moral rules which are necessary to the preservation of civil society" (Locke)[15]; liberty, but not "unlimited," consisting "only in the power of doing what we ought to will, and in not being constrained to do what we ought not to will" (Montesquieu)[16]; liberty of speech, but not of action (Kant's "argue, but obey")[17]; the liberty of the individual as against government, but not against "public opinion" or "society" (Jefferson and Paine)[18]; freedom, but under conditions of "order and moderation" (Macaulay)[19]; liberty, but not "without morality, nor morality without faith" (Tocqueville).[20]

Yet it is *On Liberty*, in defiance of all precedent, that has set the terms of the debate for our time—for people who have not read the essay, who may not have heard of it, but who have absorbed its message by cultural osmosis. In his autobiography, Mill describes it as "a kind of philosophic textbook of a single truth," and gives it a provenance worthy of such a work. Perhaps unconsciously echoing Edward Gibbon, who was inspired to write his classic in the most classical of settings, as he sat "musing amidst the ruins of the Capitol while the barefooted friars were singing vespers in the Temple of Jupiter,"[21] so Mill has the idea of *On Liberty* coming to him while he was "mounting the steps of the Capitol."[22] This, he told his wife, is the most important subject that can occupy their few remaining years, and they must "cram into it as much as possible of what we wish not to leave unsaid." It was to be their legacy to humanity, and he was confident that "it will be read and make a sensation."[23] His prediction was borne out. When the book was published four years later, after the death of his wife and as a memorial to her, it became an instant classic. With the benefit of hindsight, we might also say that it has proved to be even more influential than its author expected.

"Ideas," Lord Acton once wrote, "have a radiation and development, an ancestry and posterity of their own, in which men play the part of godfathers and godmothers more than that of legitimate parents."[24] This has been the fate of *On Liberty*. Like all classics, it has taken on a life of its own, even while it retains the unmistakable features of its paternity. *On Liberty* was radical enough in its own time, but it is, in a sense, still more radical in ours, because it seems to validate contemporary ideas about liberty which go well beyond those that Mill intended.

One of Mill's arguments, for example, for the absolute liberty of discussion is that such liberty is required for the sake of truth, for its emergence and continued vitality. About truth itself—that there is such a thing as truth, that it is finally knowable, and that it is of primary value to humanity—Mill had no doubt. He was not, in this respect, a relativist. But his doctrine lends itelf to relativism, even of an extreme kind. By making truth so dependent upon liberty— and upon the liberty of error as much as truth—it suggests that in the free marketplace of ideas, all opinions, true and false, are equal, equally valuable to society and equally worthy of promulgation. Mill himself meant only to say that society cannot presume to decide between truth and falsity, or even to lend its support to truth once that has been determined. But a later generation, deprived of the authority of society and impressed by the latitude given to error, can so relativize and "problematize" truth as to be skeptical of the very idea of truth.

Thus, postmodernists deny not only absolute truth but

contingent, partial, incremental truths. For them absolute liberty is not, as it was for Mill, the precondition of truth; rather it is the precondition for the liberation from truth itself, even from the "will to truth." In the jargon of the school, truth is "totalizing," "hegemonic," "logocentric," "phallocentric," "autocratic," "tyrannical." Mill would assuredly have been distressed by this development. But his principle of absolute liberty, which "privileges" error together with truth, cannot be absolved entirely from responsibility for it.

As truth has been relativized—absolutely relativized, so to speak—so has morality. Again, Mill himself was not a relativist in moral affairs. He firmly believed that chastity is inherently superior to promiscuity, sobriety to drunkenness, decency to indecency, altruism to self-interest. But he also firmly believed that as truth is dependent upon the absolute liberty of discussion, so morality is dependent upon a maximum amount of individuality. And as society (still less the government) should not try to promote truth or suppress error, so there should be no legal or social sanctions to promote morality or discourage immorality.

It is not always appreciated how far *On Liberty* goes in denying not only to the law but to the informal mechanisms of society any control over the individual in respect to behavior that is properly regarded as immoral but that does not harm others. Social and moral sanctions, Mill insists, are as much encroachments on liberty as legal and physical ones. So long as they do not harm others, individuals must be free to act as they like, "without hindrance, either physical or moral."[25] Acts are subject to "moral reprobation" only when they involve a "breach of duty to others," but not if they are merely evidence of "folly, or want of personal dignity and self-respect."[26] Social sanctions are called for when an individual's acts are harmful to others but do not legally violate the "constituted rights" of others; in this case the offender may be "justly punished by opinion, though not by law." But when a person's conduct affects only himself, the individual has "perfect freedom, legal and social," to do as he likes.[27]

Even the qualification regarding harm reinforces the moral neutrality of society, for it is only in the case of harm to others, not for the "good" of others, that society can properly interfere with the freedom of the individual. And harm itself is further qualified by being limited to "direct," "definite," "perceptible" harm—not such indirect harm as might come from the example of misconduct or the temptation to vice, for that example "needs not affect them unless they like."[28]

Mill's paean to individuality reflects an extraordinary optimism about human nature.

> To say that one person's desires and feelings are stronger and more various than those of another, is merely to say that he has more of the raw material of human nature, and is therefore capable, perhaps of more evil, but certainly of more good. Strong impulses are but another name for energy. Energy may be turned to bad uses; but more good may always be made of an energetic nature, than of an indolent and impassive one. Those who have most natural feeling are always those whose cultivated feelings may be made the strongest. The same strong susceptibilities which make the personal impulses vivid and powerful, are also the source from whence are generated the most passionate love of virtue, and the sternest self-control. . . . The danger which threatens human nature is not the ex-

cess, but the deficiency, of personal impulses and preferences.[29]

The argument rests on the transmutation of quantity into quality: the assumption that the larger the stock of "energy" or the "raw material of human nature," the greater the potentiality for good; that those who have "most natural feeling" also have the strongest "cultivated feelings"; that "strong susceptibilities" make for the "most passionate love of virtue"; that the danger comes not from an excess but from a deficiency of "personal impulses and preferences." This, as much as the principle of liberty, is the great novelty of Mill's argument. Most philosophers and theologians before him (and not only Calvinists, as he suggests) were wary of the raw material of human nature, finding in it at least as much potentiality for evil as for good, and therefore sought ways of refining and controlling it. They located the source of virtue not in the individual's passions, desires, impulses, feelings, or susceptibilities, but in his conscience, will, reason, forethought, and self-restraint. As a further precaution, they placed the individual within the protective custody, as it were, of family, law, religion, society, and civilization.

That *On Liberty* takes so optimistic a view of human nature is all the more remarkable in the light of Mill's other writings at that very time. In the essay "Nature," written only months before he started *On Liberty*, Mill argued that the spontaneous "impulses," "inclinations," and "instincts" of man are more likely to be bad than good, and that they can be "tamed" only by an "eminently artificial discipline." As if in direct refutation of *On Liberty*, virtue is described as not natural but unnatural:

The acquisition of virtue has in all ages been accounted a work of labour and difficulty, while the *descensus Av-*

erni on the contrary is of proverbial facility; and it assuredly requires in most persons a greater conquest over a greater number of natural inclinations to become eminently virtuous than transcendently vicious.[30]

"Transcendently vicious"—the words were tragically prophetic. For we have witnessed, in our own lifetimes, a *descensus Averni* that the Mill of *On Liberty* never dreamed of, and that even the "other Mill," as I have called him elsewhere— the author of "Nature" and the many other writings at variance with *On Liberty*—could not have foreseen. Neither of them anticipated how "transcendently vicious" individuals could be, how energetic and ingenious in exploring the lowest depravities of human nature. They could not have anticipated it because both Mills lived in a world that took much for granted. Above all, what they took for granted was a civilization that would continue to impose upon individuals the "eminently artificial discipline" that was the moral corrective to human nature. They also took for granted that those virtues that had already been acquired, by means of religion, tradition, law, and all the other resources of civilization—would continue to be valued and exercised.

Nietzsche, who took nothing for granted, least of all the virtues of self-control, self-restraint, and self-discipline, had contempt for those English moralists—that "flathead" Mill, as he called him, and that "little moralistic female" George Eliot—who thought they could secularize morality by divorcing it from Christianity. Beneath their "insipid and cowardly concept 'man' " lingers the old "cult of Christian morality." What these "moral fanatics" do not realize is how conditional their morality is on the religion they profess to discard. And it is only because of the persistence of that religion that, for the English, "morality is not yet a problem."[31]

The implication of Nietzsche's remarks was ominous. When the English would have used up the religious capital that was the source of their morality, when the divorce between religion and morality was complete, morality would indeed become a "problem." Here, too, *On Liberty* is a portent of what was to come, for it prepared the way for that divorce by placing the individual in an adversarial relationship to religion, at least in its public role. As a matter of private belief and practice, religion and the morality derived from religion are fully protected by the principle of liberty. But as soon as they impinge upon the individual from the outside, in the form of legal sanctions or social pressures, they jeopardize liberty and contribute to the evil of "social tyranny."

Mill concedes that religious and moral beliefs, once the source of bloody persecution, now produce only the "rags and remnants of persecution." But so long as such beliefs are supported by either legal or social sanctions, there is a real possibility of the revival of persecution—and if not actual persecution, then economic penalties that are as bad, for "men might as well be imprisoned, as excluded from the means of earning their bread." This is a danger so long as people have strong opinions and feelings about the beliefs of others. And it is because such opinions and feelings still abide among the "middle classes of this country" that England is "not a place of mental freedom."[32]

The distrust of strong opinions and feelings about religion and morality, the suspicion that they will promote intolerance, bigotry, even persecution, seems inconsistent with the celebration of individuality that pervades *On Liberty*. If individuality is commendable because it promotes strong opinions, feelings, desires, impulses, preferences, susceptibilities, it must also promote strong opinions, feelings, and beliefs about religion and morality. Mill cannot mean to suggest that individuality is well and good only so long as it avoids the subjects of religion and morality. In fact, he clearly has no objection to strong feelings, opinions, and beliefs directed against conventional religious and moral views. Indeed, it is one of the purposes of individuality, he insists, to permit, even encourage, the expression of heterodoxy and nonconformity, to challenge religious dogmas and defy moral conventions.

This apparent inconsistency reflects a barely concealed animus in *On Liberty* against religion, against a morality sanctioned by religion, and against a people still respectful of orthodox religion.

> What is boasted of at the present time as the revival of religion, is always, in narrow and uncultivated minds, at least as much the revival of bigotry; and where there is the strong permanent leaven of intolerance in the feelings of a people, which at all times abides in the middle classes of this country, it needs but little to provoke them into actively persecuting those whom they have never ceased to think proper objects of persecution.[33]

This animus is all the more marked because so far from there being a "revival of bigotry," let alone persecution, in England at this time, there was a significant expansion of toleration, evident in the elimination of religious tests for officeholding, membership in Parliament, and admission to the universities.* And so far from boasts of a "revival of

---

*A long footnote on the Sepoy insurrection decries the public response to it as exhibiting the "passions of a persecutor" and "the worst parts of our national character." As evidence, Mill cites the "ravings of fanatics or charlatans from the pulpit," the proposal of some Evangelicals that publicly funded schools in India be obliged to teach the Bible and that none but Christians be given public

religion," what was more often heard were complaints, even boasts, of the decline of religion. The census of 1851 proved what many had suspected, that there was a significant decrease in church attendance among both the working classes and the middle classes. There was also a conspicuous weakening of religious convictions and a growing sense of doubt and unbelief—this even before Darwin's *Origin of Species* (published shortly after *On Liberty*) made "the crisis of faith" a staple of discourse. One would not suspect, from Mill's essay, that religion was then on the defensive, that there was a flourishing secularist and anti-religious movement, and that religious institutions, doctrines, and practices displayed all the variety and eccentricity that he so much valued in other aspects of social and intellectual life.

Implicit in Mill's discussion of religion is an idea that is central to his conception of liberalism as well as to our own: the distinction between public and private. Religious beliefs and activities are respected and protected by his principle of liberty so long as they are held and practiced privately,

---

employment, and a speech by an under-secretary of state suggesting that religious toleration be limited to the toleration of Christian sects. "Who, after this imbecile display," Mill concludes, "can indulge the illusion that religious persecution has passed away, never to return?"[34] What he neglects to say is that these were untypical and unpopular sentiments. In fact, the public and Parliament were so aroused by the news of the brutal treatment of the rebels (who themselves had committed atrocities upon English soldiers) that laws were passed abolishing the East India Company, prohibiting the expropriation of land, admitting Indians to the civil service, and decreeing religious toleration in India—this at the very time that Mill was predicting the return of "religious persecution."

but they become threats to liberty as soon as they enter the public domain.

The distinction between public and private—between "other-regarding" and "self-regarding" acts, as Mill put it—is coterminous with the principle of liberty itself: it sets "the limits to the authority of society over the individual."[35] The fundamental maxim is simple enough: "Purely self-regarding misconduct cannot properly be meddled with"—and cannot be meddled with, moreover, either "in the way of prevention or punishment." Drunkenness, for example, can be restricted or punished only if the drunkard has a history of violence or if it actually causes "harm to others."[36] Mill anticipated the objection that no act is ever entirely self-regarding, but he made a valiant effort to retain the distinction between self- and other-regarding acts as much as possible. At one point he even applied it to the question of manners: "There are many acts which, being directly injurious only to the agents themselves, ought not to be legally interdicted, but which, if done publicly, are a violation of good manners, and coming thus within the category of offences against others, may rightly be prohibited."[37] He did not explain why a "violation of good manners," even in public, comes within the category of "offences against others" and is therefore illegal and punishable; nor whether such a violation requires evidence of direct and perceptible harm to others for it to warrant any social, let alone legal, prohibition; nor why drunkenness, which in public is surely a violation of good manners, cannot be "meddled with" unless it issues in harm to others. Nor did he clarify matters when he explained that "offences against others" include "offences against decency," and then abruptly terminated the discussion by saying that "it is unnecessary to dwell" on such offenses because they are only "connected indirectly" with his subject.[38]

The dividing line between public and private that Mill

found it difficult to establish in theory is by now impossible to sustain in practice. The idea that a "violation of good manners" constitutes an "offence against others" or an "offence against decency" is itself archaic. Who is to say, it is now commonly asked, what is mannerly or unmannerly, decent or indecent, offensive or inoffensive? And what is the justification, in the absence of positive harm, for punishing offensive behavior, whether by legal or social sanctions? Mill himself, in discussing conduct that may be held to be personally "blamable" but not legally punishable because it affects only the agent, goes on to say, "Whatever it is permitted to do, it must be permitted to advise to do"[39]—thus further blurring the distinction between self-regarding and other-regarding acts. In the United States today, that dictum has been amended to read: Whatever it is permitted to do, it must be permitted not only to advise others to do, but to do in public, and, moreover, to be paid by the public to so advise and so do. (This last argument is used to justify grants by the National Endowment for the Arts for performances on the stage that Mill would surely have prohibited as indecent and offensive, to say nothing of unmannerly.)

And if something is legal, is it not also moral? This is another distinction that we find difficult to sustain. Logically, of course, it is simple to distinguish between legality and morality. But in public affairs, this distinction becomes as tenuous as that between private and public. If the law deems something to be legal, who is to say that it is immoral, except the individual who is free to speak and act for himself, and only himself? In a culture that has learned the lesson of *On Liberty* all too well—that resents the "tyranny" of society, custom, and public opinion, that is profoundly suspicious of any authority suggestive of a "moral police," that has erected the highest barriers between church and state so as to prevent any intimation of intolerance or coercion—what remains to give conviction and authority to a moral code that is distinct from, and perhaps in contradiction to, the legal code? It takes a great effort of will and intellect for the individual to decide for himself that something is immoral, and to act on that belief, when the law and the institutions of the state deem it to be permissible and legal. It takes an even greater effort for parents to inculcate that belief in their children, and persuade them to act on it, when public schools and official authorities contravene that belief and authorize behavior in violation of it.

You cannot legislate morality, it is often said—and Mill would have agreed. In fact, we have done just that, and liberals are properly proud of it. The considerable body of civil rights legislation in America, prohibiting racial, sexual, and other forms of discrimination, is thoroughly moral in intention and effect. It is inspired by moral principles; it prescribes and proscribes specific forms of moral behavior; and it has changed, to a significant degree, the moral beliefs, attitudes, and practices of the public. But if morality can be legislated, so can immorality. If liberals can take satisfaction in civil rights legislation, conservatives can be distressed by laws that condone sexual promiscuity, undermine "family values," and sanction "alternative life-styles" that they find immoral.

Legislation, to be sure, for conservatives as for liberals, is a last resort. And legislation itself relies, as Machiavelli reminds us, upon morals. "For as good manners cannot subsist without good laws, so those laws cannot be put into execution without good manners" ("manners," in this context, meaning "morals").[40]* A corollary of this principle holds that if

_____

*Thomas Hobbes similarly identifies "manners" with "morals": "By manners, I mean not here decency of behaviour; as how one man should salute another, or how a man should wash his mouth,

laws are not to be too intrusive, then society must assume some responsibility for shaping public morality. Just as legal sanctions obviate (to a large extent, although not entirely) the use of force, so social sanctions obviate (again, largely, but not entirely) the use of legal sanctions.

Mill, however, and most liberals after him have called into question any relationship between morality and legality. They do not believe that law must be grounded in or even be congruent with morality. Nor do they think it proper for morality, as expressed in social sanctions, to take the place of law, to do what it may be imprudent or impractical for the law to try to do. Instead, they proscribe social sanctions together with legal sanctions, stigmatizing both as the instruments of "social tyranny." In doing so, they unwittingly invite a worse tyranny, for legislation may then be called upon to do what society would otherwise have done less obtrusively and more benignly.

One of the paradoxes of contemporary liberalism is that it has become increasingly libertarian in moral affairs and at the same time increasingly *dirigiste* in economic affairs. In the moral realm, the individual is as close to being "sovereign"—or, we would now say, "autonomous"—as Mill could have desired. In the economic realm, however, the state exercises a degree of control at least the equal of the "social tyranny" that he so feared.

It is common to remark upon the great difference between nineteenth-century laissez-faire liberalism and twentieth-century social-welfare liberalism. The difference can be exaggerated: laissez-faireism was never as rigorous or sys-

---

or pick his teeth before company, and such other points of the *small morals*; but those qualities of mankind that concern their living together in peace and unity."[41]

tematic as was once thought; and the social-welfare state, with the demise of communism and the discrediting of socialism, is now on the defensive if not in retreat. But with all due qualifications, the distinction between the two modes of liberalism is real and significant. No less real and significant is the disjunction within contemporary liberalism between the moral and the economic realms.

Here, too, the problem may be seen in embryo in *On Liberty*, although Mill made a determined, if not entirely persuasive, effort to minimize it. "Trade is a social act," he pronounced, therefore in principle falling within the province of society.[42] Restraints on trade are "evil" insofar as they are restraints, but they are "wrong" only if they do not produce the desired results. Thus the government, Mill finds, can properly intervene to prevent the adulteration of products or assure the health and safety of workers in dangerous industries. But other restraints, such as temperance laws or restrictions on the sale of poisons, are a violation of liberty because they infringe on the liberty of the buyer rather than the producer.

The logical difficulties here are obvious. Why is it a violation of the principle of liberty to restrain the buyer but not the producer? Why should the sale of adulterated food be prohibited but not the sale of poison? If poisons require only proper labeling and a registry of sale but not medical prescription, why are these conditions not sufficient for adulterated products? Whatever the inconsistencies in Mill's argument, however, his purpose is clear: to limit the role of government, on grounds of expediency as well as liberty. His guiding rules for such limitations are equally clear. The government should not intervene "when the thing to be done is likely to be better done by individuals than by the government"; when individuals may not do it as well but "it is nevertheless desirable that it be done by them, rather than by the government, as a means to their own mental education"; and when government intervention would contribute to "the great evil of adding unnecessarily to its power." These conditions, Mill specifies, militate against government control of roads, railways, banks, large companies, universities, and the like, even if that would make for greater efficiency. Indeed, the evil would be all the greater the more efficient the government might be, for if the government were to exercise such control, no amount of freedom of the press or popular government would make England or any other country "free otherwise than in name."[43]*

Contemporary liberalism has taken Mill's dictum "Trade is a social act" and carried it to an extreme. Where Mill severely restricts the role of government in trade, thus minimizing the disparity between the moral and economic spheres, liberals today have conspicuously enlarged the gap by giving the government ever increasing powers in economic affairs while endowing the individual with ever greater autonomy in moral affairs. More than a quarter of a century ago, the English jurist Lord Devlin characterized this as a combination of "physical paternalism and moral individualism."[45] Today, a more accurate formula would be "social paternalism and moral individualism," for the scope of government intervention has been extended from physical to social is-

---

*In spite of this unambiguous statement, Mill is sometimes described as a socialist. This claim is based on some extremely equivocal passages in his *Political Economy* (most of them inserted on the insistence of his wife and against his own judgment, as he himself said), and on a misreading of his last uncompleted essays published posthumously under the title *Chapters on Socialism*. It is often assumed, perhaps on the basis of the title alone, that these essays were an argument in favor of socialism; in fact they are a sustained critique of it.[44]

sues—from matters affecting health and safety, wages and hours, industry and the environment, to such concerns as racial integration, sexual equality, affirmative action, multicultural education, and the like. To some liberals, these social goals seem so compelling as to require a suspension of even the most absolute of liberties, the liberty of speech. Thus some favor the prohibition of "hate speech"—speech derogatory of minorities—while adamantly defending the freedom of obscene, pornographic, or blasphemous speech. Indeed, obscene, pornographic, and blasphemous acts may be subsumed under the category of "symbolic speech" and thus enjoy all the liberty adhering to speech, while "hate speech" may be prosecuted as a violation of civil rights.

By now, this combination—and disjunction—of "paternalism" and "individualism" is so familiar and so embedded in law and custom that liberals are rarely troubled by it. It has become a fact of life, one of the many "cultural contradictions" of modernity that are no longer seen as "problems" because they have attained the status of "conditions." Yet it is a problem, because it raises fundamental questions about the principle of liberty that is at the heart of modern liberalism.

It is not only the contradictions themselves that are troublesome; it is the assumptions underlying them. Why is it proper for the government to prohibit insalubrious foods but not sadistic movies, to control the pollution of the environment but not of the culture, to prevent racial segregation but not moral degradation? Is there not a double standard of values and priorities implicit here? And what is the significance of that double standard?

Does it mean that the physical, material, and social welfare of the people is deemed to be so much more important than their moral, cultural, and spiritual welfare as to justify the suspension of the principle of liberty in the former cases? Or that individuals are competent to understand and protect their moral, cultural, and spiritual interests but not their physical, material, and social interests? What conception of human nature is involved in this disjunction? What conception of the good society and the good life?

Again, Mill himself did not intend to advocate so complete a double standard, let alone so radical an inversion of values. He himself put a higher value and priority on moral goods than on material ones. This is why his book on political economy argues against an infinitely expanding economy and in favor of a "stationary" one that would limit material acquisitiveness and competition. It is also why *On Liberty* proposes to give the individual complete control over moral affairs, because only thus would he fully develop his moral faculties—that is, his higher, better faculties.

The unintended implications of *On Liberty*, however, are very different. By leaving morality and the culture entirely within the province of the individual, by removing them from the public domain, by denying to them any special attention or protection on the part of society or the state— by making them seem, in short, unproblematic—Mill unwittingly leaves the impression that they are less important, less urgent, than those physical, material, and social concerns that are problematic and do require the intervention of society and the state. This is not a logical consequence of his doctrine, but it is a plausible reading of it. One might reason, as Mill himself did, that the most important affairs are best left to the individual. But one could equally well conclude that if the government feels obliged to curtail liberty in order to protect the individual from tainted food but not from depraved literature, it is because tainted food is a more serious matter than depraved literature.

Mill would never have said, "No one has ever been corrupted by a book."* He had too high a regard for books to

_____

*Nor would Milton. His argument in *Areopagitica* is that it is precisely because of the potency of books that one must not suppress be so dismissive of their moral—or immoral—effects. But he made it possible, and plausible, for others to take that view, to think that smog and insecticides are perilous enough to call for restrictions on liberty, but that pornography and obscenity are not; or that the Surgeon General can properly compel cigarette packages to carry a warning declaring them hazardous to health, but that the Attorney General cannot authorize a label on obscene recordings declaring them deleterious to the soul. As one wit has said, it is now permissible for a performer to masturbate on the stage, but only if he or she is paid the minimum wage.

Liberalism has come a long way from *On Liberty*. But some of its current problems—its paradoxes and contradictions, excesses and limitations—lie in the principle of liberty enunciated in that work. Mill insisted that he was not dealing with liberty as a political doctrine. Yet it is obvious that the polity cannot be divorced from the ethos that sustains it, and that the principle of liberty has political as well as ethical implications that mark a decisive break with an earlier mode of liberalism.

That older tradition was appreciative of the ideas of lib-

---

them—unless, to be sure, they are "impious or evil," or inimical to "faith or manners."

> I deny not, but that it is of greatest concernment in the Church and Commonwealth, to have a vigilant eye how books demean themselves, as well as men; and thereafter to confine, imprison, and do sharpest justice on them as malefactors. For books are not absolutely dead things, but do contain a potency of life in them to be as active as that soul was whose progeny they are; nay, they do preserve as in a vial the purest efficacy and extraction of that living intellect that bred them.[46]

erty and individuality, but in a context that made liberty
consonant with the common good and individuality with the
commonality of interests in the commonwealth. This was
what was meant by "republican virtue" and "civic virtue,"
"social sympathy" and "social morality." By means of some
such common denominator, liberty was to be reconciled with
morality and the individual with society and the polity.

In Enlightenment France, in Whig England, and in republican America, the message was the same: Liberty, but
not in excess and always in conjunction with virtue. Montesquieu expressed it best: "Virtue in a republic is a most simple
thing: it is a love of the republic. . . . The natural place of
virtue is near to liberty; but it is not nearer to excessive
liberty than to servitude."[47] Even the Founding Fathers,
committed to the "new science of politics"—the theory that
"opposite and rival interests" can best sustain republican
government—recognized the importance of virtue, both in
their leaders and in the people.

> The aim of every political constitution is or ought to be
> first to obtain for rulers men who possess most wisdom
> to discern, and most virtue to pursue, the common good
> of the society; and in the next place, to take the most
> effectual precautions for keeping them virtuous, whilst
> they continue to hold their public trust.[48]

> I go on this great republican principle, that the people
> will have virtue and intelligence to select men of virtue
> and wisdom. . . . To suppose that any form of govern-
> ment will secure liberty or happiness without any virtue
> in the people, is a chimerical idea.[49]

Tocqueville, writing about America but having in mind
all those countries (notably his own) that would inevitably

follow America along the path of democracy, was especially
alert to the dangers of excessive individuality—"individualism," as he called it. That "novel expression," he explained,
derives from a "novel idea": not selfishness (*égoïsme*) in the
old sense, which is "a passionate and exaggerated love of
self," but "a mature and calm feeling" which disposes every
individual to sever himself from society. Originating with
democracy and thriving on equality, individualism saps the
"virtues of public life" and eventually of private life as well.[50]
Its effect, however, might be mitigated by private associations mediating between the individual and the state, and by
religion, which, although not part of the American government, is "the first of their political institutions."[51]

In dramatic contrast to Mill, Tocqueville saw religion
not as the potential adversary of liberty but as its ally. Because religion has to be "believed without discussion," it
removes from the individual intellect "many of the most
important of human opinions." Thus it counteracts the intellectual solipsism of Americans, their habit of "fixing the
standard of their judgment in themselves alone."[52] It also
serves as the bulwark of morality, which is the prerequisite
of liberty.

> Liberty requires religion as its companion in all its bat-
> tles and its triumphs, as the cradle of its infancy and
> the divine source of its claims. It considers religion as
> the safeguard of morality, and morality as the best secu-
> rity of law and the surest pledge of the duration of
> freedom.[53]

> Despotism may govern without faith, but liberty cannot.
> Religion . . . is more needed in democratic republics
> than in any others. How is it possible that society should
> escape destruction if the moral tie is not strengthened
> in proportion as the political tie is relaxed? And what

can be done with a people who are their own masters if they are not submissive to the Deity?[54]*

It would have come as a surprise to Mill, but not to Tocqueville, that the recent liberation of the Soviet Union and Eastern Europe was accompanied, if not in good measure caused, by the revival of religion—and religion not purely as a matter of private belief (totalitarianism never entirely succeeded in suppressing that) but as, in Tocqueville's words, "the first of their political institutions."

In Tocqueville and the Founding Fathers one finds a mode of liberalism that antedates *On Liberty* and that survives today as an alternative or corrective to it. One may also find it in Mill himself, the "other Mill," whose writings before as well as after *On Liberty* express views very different from the "one very simple principle" of that book.[56] Indeed, he denied that social affairs could be understood in terms of any single or simple principle.[57]

It is this Mill who said that man should be encouraged to "use his own judgment" but not to "*trust* solely to his own judgment"[58]; that there are "fundamental principles" that men are agreed in "holding sacred" and "above discussion"[59]; that morality can be promoted by "education and opinion," "laws and social arrangements"[60]; that the sign of an "advancing civilization" is the removal of man from a

---

*Washington quite agreed:

> Of all the dispositions and habits which lead to political prosperity, religion and morality are indispensable supports. In vain would that man claim the tribute of patriotism who should labor to subvert these great pillars of human happiness, these firmest props of the duties of men and citizens.[55]

state of "savage independence" and "miserable individuality"[61]; that "government exists for all purposes whatever that are for man's good: and that the highest and most important of these purposes is the improvement of man himself as a moral and intelligent being."[62]

It is this Mill, too, whose criticism of the *philosophes* anticipated the criticism that could be made of *On Liberty*. The mistake of the *philosophes*, he explained, was "unsettling everything which was still considered settled," uprooting whatever reverence people still felt for anything above them and undermining their respect for "the limits which custom and prescription had set to the indulgence of each man's fancies or inclinations." Above all, they failed to see that society rests on a "host of civilizing and restraining influences" that curb man's "self-will and love of independence." These influences derive from a system of education, beginning in infancy and continuing throughout life, which has as its "main and incessant ingredient" the inculcation of a "restraining discipline." The purpose of that discipline is to foster in every individual the habit and power of "subordinating his personal impulses and aims" to the ends of society, and "controlling in himself all the feelings" liable to militate against those ends. Without such a discipline, no polity could sustain itself.

> Whenever and in proportion as the strictness of the restraining discipline was relaxed, the natural tendency of mankind to anarchy reasserted itself; the state became disorganized from within; mutual conflict for selfish ends neutralized the energies which were required to keep up the contest against natural causes of evil; and the nation, after a longer or briefer interval of progressive decline, became either the slave of a despotism, or the prey of a foreign invader.[63]*

---

*Lest it be thought that these were the sentiments of a callow youth

. . .

One can only speculate on the reasons for the existence (sometimes the coexistence) of the "two Mills." But it is easier to explain why the Mill of *On Liberty* has come to overshadow the "other Mill." "One very simple principle" is always more seductive than a complicated, nuanced set of principles. And this particular principle is all the more appealing because it conforms to the image of the modern, liberated, autonomous, "authentic" individual.

It is also especially compelling at times of crisis, when liberty itself is in jeopardy. With the rise of communism and Nazism, many liberals, normally inclined to a moderate, pluralistic, pragmatic view of liberty, were persuaded that the only security against an absolutistic regime was an absolute principle of liberty. Anything less appeared incommensurate with the enormity of the evil. Totalitarianism, they believed, could be effectively opposed only by an ideology as total and uncompromising as the enemy with whom they were contending. Against absolute despotism the only adequate response seemed to be absolute liberty.

This was—and still is—the psychological basis of the "slippery slope" argument. Any deviation from absolute liberty is seen as a capitulation to tyranny, any restriction on por-

---

discarded by the mature Mill, it should be noted that he reprinted these passages repeatedly, with slight changes of wording suggesting a careful rereading. They first appeared in his essay on Coleridge in the *London and Westminster Review* in 1840. They were reprinted in his *System of Logic* in 1843, and altered slightly in the third edition of 1851, where "the restraining discipline" (in the quotation above) replaced the original wording: "this discipline." This emendation was preserved when the essay as a whole was republished in the first volume of *Dissertations and Discussions* in 1859, the same year as *On Liberty.*

nography as a mortal blow to free speech. This is the argument used by liberals in support of government subsidies for such "art" as the photograph of a crucifix submerged in urine, the painting of Christ as a drug addict with a needle in his arm, or a sexual performance compared with which the old striptease is positively puritanical. Yet the same liberals who advocate the largest freedom for artists (including the freedom to be subsidized) also tend to support, in the name of the same freedom, the strictest separation of church and state—with the curious result that the photograph of a crucifix immersed in urine can be exhibited in a public school, but a crucifix not immersed in urine cannot be exhibited.

Such absurdities point to a more serious problem: the tendency of absolute liberty to subvert the very liberty it seeks to preserve. By making particular liberties dependent on an absolute principle of liberty, by invalidating all those other principles—history, custom, law, interest, opinion, religion—which have traditionally served to support particular liberties, the absolute principle discredits these particular liberties together with the principles upon which they are based. So far from making liberty absolutely secure, the absolutistic doctrine may have the unwitting effect of depriving specific liberties, including the most basic ones, of the security they enjoy under more traditional, modest auspices. And when that absolute principle proves inadequate to the exigencies of social life, it is abandoned absolutely, replaced not by a more moderate form of liberty but by an immoderate form of government control. This is the source of the disjunction between individualism and paternalism that is so conspicuous a feature of contemporary liberalism.

The absolute principle of liberty has another perverse effect. By this standard, distinctions of degree become unimportant. Any liberty that falls short of it is seen as fatally flawed. And any society that is liberal in the traditional, non-absolutist sense is deemed to be as illiberal and illegitimate as a despotic society. This is the logic that informs the Marxist critique of liberalism as a form of "repressive tolerance," and the postmodernist critique of all societies, including the most liberal, as "tyrannical" and "authoritarian."

Those who have experienced the tyranny of totalitarianism can appreciate how very different that is from the "social tyranny" of liberal democracy. They can also appreciate the dangers of an absolute principle of liberty that gives little positive, legal, institutional support for those private and public virtues—"republican virtues" or "civic virtues"—required of a liberal democracy. We have just such a testament from the leader of a newly liberated country who is himself not only an unexceptionable liberal but also a distinguished writer and intellectual.

It was only two years after his triumphal visit to the United States, when he informed an enthusiastic Congress that "Consciousness precedes Being, and not the other way around,"[64] that Václav Havel, the president of Czechoslovakia, reflected on the unanticipated consequences of liberty itself—a liberty that threatened to liberate his countrymen not only from the tyranny of communism but from the constraints of morality.

> The return of freedom to a place that became morally unhinged has produced something that it clearly had to produce, and therefore something we might have expected. But it has turned out to be far more serious than anyone could have predicted: an enormous and blindingly visible explosion of every imaginable human vice. A wide range of questionable or at least ambivalent human tendencies, quietly encouraged over the years and, at the same time, quietly pressed to serve the daily operation of the totalitarian system, has suddenly been

liberated, as it were, from its straitjacket and given free rein at last. The authoritarian regime imposed a certain order—if that is the right expression for it—on these vices (and in doing so "legitimized" them, in a sense). This order has now been broken down, but a new order that would limit rather than exploit these vices, an order based on a freely accepted responsibility to and for the whole of society, has not yet been built, nor could it have been, for such an order takes years to develop and cultivate.

And thus we are witnesses to a bizarre state of affairs: society has freed itself, true, but in some ways it behaves worse than when it was in chains.[65]

Liberals have always known that absolute power tends to corrupt absolutely. Like Havel, we are now discovering that absolute liberty also tends to corrupt absolutely. A liberty that is divorced from tradition and convention, from morality and religion, that makes the individual the sole repository and arbiter of all values and puts him in an adversarial relationship to society and the state—such a liberty is a grave peril to liberalism itself. For when that liberty is found wanting, when it violates the moral sense of the community or is incompatible with the legitimate demands of society, there is no moderating principle to take its place, no resting place between the wild gyrations of libertarianism and paternalism.

Fortunately, we have another liberal tradition to repair to, that of Montesquieu, the Founding Fathers, Tocqueville, and the "other Mill." It is there that we may find a liberalism "properly understood" that will protect us from both the horrors of absolute power and the excesses of absolute liberty.

V

The Dark and Bloody Crossroads Where Nationalism and Religion Meet

IT WAS IN A FRESHMAN history course shortly after the outbreak of the Second World War that I was formally introduced to the concept of nationalism. The war, the professor informed us, was the last gasp of nationalism, nationalism in its death throes. Nationalism had been a nineteenth-century phenomenon, the romantic by-product of the nation-state in its prime. It had barely survived the First World War, and the Second would surely bring it to an end, together with those other obsolete institutions, the nation-state and capitalism. The professor, a scholar of much distinction, spoke with great authority, for he had personal as well as professional knowledge of his subject; as a recent German émigré, he possessed intimate, tragic experience of that anachronism known as nationalism.

This was my introduction, not only to nationalism but to

the kind of cognitive dissonance—the discrepancy between reality and ideology—that only truly learned and clever people can achieve. At the end of the war, another eminent historian, E. H. Carr, having just witnessed the most violent assault by an aggressive nationalism turned back by the heroic efforts and sacrifices of a defensive nationalism, predicted the imminent demise of nationalism and of nationality itself. America, he explained, was not so much a nation as a melting pot. The Soviet Union had demonstrated a "comprehensive Soviet allegiance" that overrode the multiplicity of its "component nations." In Asia, the demand for self-determination might still be heard, though "more faintly and less confidently than of late." And small nations would survive, if they did, "only as an anomaly and an anachronism."[1] (Within a year of this prediction, India was an independent nation; the next year, Pakistan followed suit; and the year after that, the state of Israel was created.)

Recently, the argument has taken a new turn, for it is now not only the future of nationalism and nationality that is denied but their past as well. Again, it testifies to a peculiarly intellectual perversity that this view should have been most forcibly expressed by an American at the very time that the United States was enthusiastically celebrating its bicentenary—and by a historian whose specialty is the history of another nation. It was in 1976 that Theodore Zeldin called upon his colleagues to liberate themselves from the "tyrannies" that had held them in bondage: chronology, causation, and collectivity—the last including the idea of the nation.[2] Six years later, he repeated his call for liberation: "A national perspective cannot be sustained in historical study much longer." There is not and never was any such thing as "national identity," because nations are not, contrary to the common impression, distinct entities. "All our instincts tell us that there is something different between a German and an Italian, but then all our instincts tell us that the earth is flat."[3]* (The first of these pronouncements appeared just before the publication of the second volume of Zeldin's highly acclaimed history of France, and the second at the same time as his next book, *The French*.)[5]

This is the new "problematic" of nationalism: the "demystification" and "demythicization" of nationalism, and thus of the nation itself. Nationalism, it is said, was fostered throughout the nineteenth century and until the present by a series of "cultural artifacts" that sustain the "imagined communities" we call nations or nationalities. Benedict Anderson, who coined the now modish term "imagined communities," does not intend it in any invidious sense. Communities are "imagined" not because they are contrived or false, but rather because the members of any nation cannot possibly know one another and therefore relate to one another in "the image of their communion."[6] Similarly, "cultural artifacts" are not artificially "fabricated" but rather the "spontaneous distillation" of complex historical forces; thus they command "profound emotional legitimacy." (Some newer nationalities, to be sure, are "pirated" versions of the

---

*It is curious to find this idea echoed by Michael Oakeshott, who rejects nationality as an organizing principle in the writing of history on the ground that it reflects a "practical" or "present-minded" approach to the past. "We may be offered 'A History of France,' but only if its author has abandoned the engagement of an historian in favour of that of an ideologue or a mythologist shall we find in it an identity—*La Nation* or *La France*—to which the differences that compose the story are attributed."[4] One wonders whether Oakeshott would have found "A History of England" quite so ideological or mythical.

old ones, modeled on the old and therefore "imagined" in a mechanical, derivative way.[7])

Anderson's is a subtle and nuanced version of this theory. More often, it appears in a coarser form, which emphasizes the artificial, manufactured character of the artifacts that generate and sustain nationalism. At the same time that Anderson introduced the idea of imagined communities, Eric Hobsbawm coined another term that became even more popular: "invented traditions." These traditions, as Hobsbawm describes them, are for the most part "conscious and deliberate" creations designed for ideological purposes, "exercises in social engineering" intended to create a continuity with the past that is "largely factitious."[8]

By now we have an abundant literature devoted to the myths, symbols, rituals, festivals, ceremonials, souvenirs, and other "inventions" meant to stimulate—and simulate—nationalist sentiments and sensibilities. The effect, if not the purpose, of all this is to "problematize" nationalism and "demystify" nationality—which is to say, to belittle nationalism and belie nationality. It is not surprising to find Hobsbawm, in his latest book on the subject, assuring us that nationalism "is no longer a major vector of historical development," that it is of "declining historical significance."[9] This was written in 1990, at the very time that the dissolution of the Soviet empire was generating powerful nationalist movements, when the Middle East was experiencing even more nationalist turmoil than usual, and when the number of states in the United Nations was at an all-time high, and threatening, every day, to become even higher.

Nationalism induces this kind of cognitive dissonance, not only among Marxists like Hobsbawm, who have a stake in the theory of the "withering away of the state" (and of the nation—the "workers of the world" have no nation), but also among liberals and some conservatives. Liberals find it difficult to credit the fact, and the force, of nationalism because it violates some of their most cherished assumptions: that people are rational individuals with universal interests and aspirations; that nations are nothing more than an aggregate of individuals; and that nationalism is irrational, parochial, and retrograde. (A neo-liberal version of this doctrine has the nation-state being superseded by a "civil society" dominated by individuals, groups, and communities responsive to local and particular rather than national concerns.)

Some conservatives are respectful of nationalism, on the Burkean principle that the nation is one of the "contracts" that bind together "those who are living, those who are dead, and those who are yet to be born." But other conservatives, of a libertarian disposition, are distrustful of nationalism, partly because of their hostility to the state, and partly because of their suspicion of any kind of ideology or zealotry. Moreover, both liberals and conservatives have good reason to will away nationalism, to prefer that it not exist. After the experience of Nazism, it is quite understandable that the benign forms of nationalism should be discredited together with the malign forms.

If nationalism invites this denial of reality, religion does still more, and for some of the same reasons—because it defies the Enlightenment principles of rationalism, universalism, secularism, materialism. I am speaking now of religion not as a private, personal belief—this the enlightened world can tolerate as an individual idiosyncrasy protected by the principle of liberty. What is less tolerable, in this view, is religion as an organized, institutional force that presumes to impinge on the public realm. Religion in this sense is taken to be as obsolete as nationalism itself. After all, it was

more than two centuries ago that the *philosophes* assured us
that the last priest would be strangled in the entrails of the
last king (or was it the other way around?).

Yet here we are, in defiance of all expectations, confronting a lethal combination of nationalism and religion—and
not in one region but all over the globe. The "national question," which not only Marxists but most enlightened intellectuals (again, conservatives as well as liberals) had consigned
to the ash can of history, is threatening to become *the* question of the present and future. And the national question,
it is also becoming obvious, is intimately associated with religion. How else are we to understand what is happening in
the Middle East (and not only the Arab-Israeli conflict but
religious conflicts within the Arab world), or in the former
Soviet empire, or in what was once Greater India, or in
Yugoslavia, or—let us not forget just because it is so tragically familiar—in Northern Ireland? These are the realities
of our world, the "bloody crossroads" where nationalism and
religion meet.[10]

These realities, too, have eluded most historians. If my
German-refugee history professor could be so blithely dismissive of nationalism, it is no wonder that others have been
equally dismissive—or, rather, oblivious—of the religious
component in nationalism. There are major works on nationalism, by historians of great distinction (and, again, by
conservatives as well as liberals), that hardly mention religion
as a significant factor in its history.[11] A recently published
Encyclopedia of Nationalism has entries on "Cultural Nationalism," "Dynastic Nationalism," "Economic Nationalism,"
"Humanitarian Nationalism," "Integral Nationalism," even
"Music and Nationalism," but nothing on "Religious Nationalism" or "Religion and Nationalism." (It does have
"Nationalism as a Religion," but "religion" here is used metaphorically, to suggest the emotive nature of nationalism.)[12]

Even the apparent exceptions prove the rule. A recent

work by Linda Colley has British (not merely English) nationalism forged in the crucible of war and religion—and war, more often than not, in the service of religion. It was Protestantism in the eighteenth century that made "the invention of Great Britain possible."* In the Victorian period, the Empire was seen as proof of Britain's "Providential destiny," testimony to its status as "the Protestant Israel." But that was then. Now, Colley concludes, with the decline of Protestantism as a vital part of British culture and the absence of any Catholic enemy in Europe—indeed, with Britain committed to the European Community—the identity of Britons and their sense of nationalism is in "doubt and disarray."[14] At this point, Colley joins most of her colleagues, who find little religion and less nationalism in the world today. (Colley excludes Ireland from her book. Had she included it, she might have discovered more evidence of both.)

Another notable exception is Conor Cruise O'Brien, who finds a surfeit of nationalism and religion in the contemporary world. Most of his *God Land* deals with the history of nationalist-cum-religious sentiments, starting with the Bible and going through the Reformation, Puritan America, and the French Revolution. Only the last chapter, "God Land Now," deals with the present, and there O'Brien testifies both to the enduring power of religious nationalism (or nationalist religion) and to his distrust of most forms of it. In

---

*The religious component in English nationalism is sometimes traced further back, to the English Reformation, when Henry VIII was declared to be Supreme Head of the Church. One historian has gone so far as to say, "The birth of the English nation was not the birth of a nation; it was the birth of the nations, the birth of nationalism."[13] But this is a distinctly minority point of view. The more common view has nationalism originating in the French Revolution, thus giving it an entirely secular character.

Latin America, nationalism and liberation theology merge to produce a "holy nationalism" comparable to that of the early Puritans, while in the United States, nationalism hovers between the idea of a "holy nation," which still retains some sense (although a too feeble one) of a nation under God, and the more extreme form of "deified nation," which recognizes no being or law superior to itself. To a "professed agnostic" like himself, both of these are cause for alarm—although less alarming, O'Brien adds, than a nationalism entirely in the service of technology. His own preference is for a nationalism that incorporates the least zealous form of religion, a "chosen people" whose national pride is mitigated by humility before God—or, better yet, Abraham Lincoln's version, "this almost chosen people." "That 'almost,'" O'Brien concludes, "is not the least precious part of your [the United States'] great heritage."[15]

There is a good deal of justification for the neglect of religion in respect to the nationalist movements of the nineteenth century, which were overwhelmingly secular—indeed, in some instances anti-religious, making a conscious effort to displace religion, particularly the universalistic religion of Catholicism, as the primary allegiance of men. The nineteenth-century French historian Jules Michelet said that the idea of the nation arose to fill the immeasurable abyss left by the extinction of the idea of God. This was certainly true of the nationalism generated by the French Revolution in France itself, although perhaps not of the nationalism inspired in subject nations resisting the encroachments of the Napoleonic regime. It was true of Italian nationalism, which was a secularist revolt against the domination of the papacy as well as a nationalist revolt against Austria. And it was true of Germany, where nationalism expressed itself in the union of Protestants and Catholics.

Even in Ireland in the nineteenth century, nationalism appealed to political rather than religious sentiments. The Young Irelanders, the Fenians, of the mid-nineteenth century, were republicans and democrats more than Catholics, and the militant Home Rulers of the late nineteenth century (including Parnell) were as often as not Protestants. By the early twentieth century, however, the vision of a united, independent Ireland foundered on the reality of the Protestant-Catholic conflict, which led to the division of Ireland after the war—a solution that solved nothing and that continues to bedevil England and Ireland alike.

As in Ireland, so in other parts of the world, religion began to emerge, after the First World War and even more after the Second, as a prime mover of nationalism. Yet historians, sociologists, political scientists, even journalists, have not been properly appreciative of this, partly because of their ideological predisposition against religion (their inability to take it seriously as a force in modernity), partly because of their professional blinders (their commitment to "scientific" explanations of "unscientific" phenomena). For them, nationalism, insofar as it persists contrary to all rational expectations, does so as the by-product of modernization.[16] And religion, insofar as it plays a part in nationalism, does so as a stratagem of social and political elites who are themselves secularists but use the rhetoric of religion to mobilize the populace and assure their allegiance. Even among the populace, one eminent sociologist finds little evidence of either religious or nationalist sentiments in "day-to-day life."[17] Another, after asserting that nationalism does not have "any very deep roots in the human psyche," goes on to exclaim upon the "fascinating relationship between the Reformation and nationalism." But the Reformation he has in mind has to do with "literacy and scripturalism," "priestless unitarianism," and "individualism"—a Reformation, in short, that is not so much religious as anti-clerical and secularist.[18]

This view of modernity is sophisticated and plausible. But it hardly does justice to the experiences of the last half century, let alone to more recent events: the Arab-Israeli wars and the *intifada* that is war by other means; the bloody conflicts between Hindus and Muslims in India; the atrocities committed by Iraq against the Shiites and by the Serbs against the Muslims in Bosnia. We are appalled to hear of the Serbian policy of "ethnic cleansing." But that is a euphemism—not only the word "cleansing," but the word "ethnic." In this case (as in so many others), ethnic means nothing more or less than religious. It used to be said that language is the distinctive criterion of nationality. Yet Serbs, Croats, and Bosnian Muslims share a language. What they do not share is a religion. And what we have been witnessing is simple, old-fashioned religious persecution.

Much has been said of the "End of History" thesis, but perhaps not enough about one aspect of it that is all too typical of contemporary thinking. Francis Fukuyama has been criticized for the ease with which he dismisses nationalism as a significant force in history. But what has not been sufficiently recognized is that in dismissing nationalism, he also dismisses religion. In his original article, religion and nationalism appear as the two remaining "contradictions" in liberal society. These, we are assured, have no "universal significance," because nationalism persists only in the Third World or in "post-historical" parts of Europe like Northern Ireland, and religion is a problem only in the form of fundamentalism.[19]

His book *The End of History and the Last Man* elaborates upon this thesis. "The desire for recognition based on nationality or race," Fukuyama explains, "is not a rational one."[20] Nor, apparently, is the desire for recognition based on religion, for he goes on to draw a parallel between nationalism and religion. He reminds us of the religious wars of the sixteenth century, when Europe squandered its wealth in the cause of religious fanaticism. In reaction against that waste of resources and out of sheer economic self-interest, religion was finally "taught to be tolerant" and "relegated to the sphere of private life." Thus it came about that *"liberalism vanquished religion in Europe"* (his italics). The same will happen to nationalism: "Nationalism can be defanged and modernized like religion." And domesticated and privatized as well: "The French can continue to savor their wines and the Germans their sausages, but this will all be done within the sphere of private life alone."[21]

Fukuyama, like his mentor Hegel, takes the long view. In that long view, nationalism has no "universal significance." It is a blip on the panorama of history, a history that has come to an end without the knowledge of its victims.

Lionel Trilling once wrote, of other historians who prided themselves on taking the "long view," that " 'the long view' is the falsest historical view of all"; seen from a sufficient distance, "the corpse and hacked limbs are not so very terrible, and eventually they even begin to compose themselves into a 'meaningful pattern.' "[22] Those words were written over fifty years ago, when many enlightened, sophisticated liberals were taking a "long view" of Nazism and communism, looking upon Nazism as an ugly but ephemeral excrescence on the face of history, and communism as an ideal marred by an unsightly but fortunately temporary blemish, rather like teenage acne, that would disappear with maturity. Both of these anomalies, as liberals then thought them, have now been vanquished, after exacting a cost in death and suffering that defies calculation and even comprehension. But many of us have yet to come to terms with the larger, "universal" significance of these phenomena—not with Nazism and communism as such, but with the "liberal imagination" that could not see them for what they were because it itself has so enlightened, rational, progressive, and ultimately narrow a view of human nature.

It is this view of human nature that makes it difficult to believe that nationalism and religion, in one form or another, in one degree or another, for good and bad, will be with us for the foreseeable future. (Not, perhaps, until the end of history, but then some of us are too unimaginative to conceive of such an end.) And it is the same view of human nature that makes it difficult to distinguish the various degrees and forms of nationalism and to pass judgment upon them.

The liberal imagination was not always so constrained. In the heyday of what has been called "liberal nationalism"—the nationalism of liberation rather than domination—the preeminent liberal, John Stuart Mill, made just such distinctions and judgments. Mill was a great champion of nationalism, which he saw as the corollary of liberalism and democracy. "Where the sentiment of nationality exists in any force, there is a *prima facie* case for uniting all the members of the nationality under the same government, and a government to themselves apart. This is merely saying that the question of government ought to be decided by the governed." But the desire for unity and independence could be satisfied only under specific conditions: the country had to be "ripe for free institutions"; there had to be no "geographical hindrances" to unity (as in Hungary, for example, where the different nationalities were so intermingled that they had to "reconcile themselves to living together under equal rights and laws"); and the people had to meet one "purely moral and social consideration"—they had to have attained a level of civilization that made it advantageous for them to be independent. The last criterion disqualified those "inferior and more backward" peoples (such as the Bretons and

Basques, the Welsh and Scottish Highlanders) who live amid "highly civilized and cultivated" peoples and who should be pleased to be absorbed into those higher nationalities.[23]

Mill's three points were later superseded by Woodrow Wilson's Fourteen Points, and a qualified principle of nationality by an unqualified "right" of "self-determination." The result has been a catastrophic failure of political imagination and political candor—an inability to think and speak realistically about peoples and nations, about what they might desire and what they are capable of achieving, about their will and capacity for free institutions, above all, about that ultimate "moral and social consideration," their level of civilization. It is almost impossible today to speak of higher and lower civilizations, let alone of "inferior and more backward" peoples. It has even become difficult to speak candidly about the "free institutions" required of those aspiring to self-determination, institutions designed to assure religious toleration, minority representation, and respect for ethnic differences. Now that such conditions are more pertinent than ever—certainly far more than in Mill's time—we are more than ever inhibited about discussing them. We cannot say what has become so painfully obvious: Not all countries are disposed or committed to free institutions. Not all nationalities are worthy of respect and recognition. Not all peoples have a "right" to independence and self-determination. In the post–Cold War world, as before, there is no moral equivalence among nations—or among would-be nations.

These are the paradoxical realities of our time. In an international world, nationalism is rife. And in a secular world, religion is alive and well—and not only the kind of religion that is denigrated as "fundamentalist," but the time-honored religions that continue to command intellectual respect as well as pious devotion. There is no point denying these realities, and every reason to admit them, if only to be realistic in trying to meliorate and conciliate them in the interests of a humane, pacific, civil order.

Being realistic means respecting the power and passion of nationalism even as we try to mitigate its excesses. There is something pathetic in the attempt to counteract a virulent nationalism with a vapid internationalism, or to substitute an artificial, bureaucratic "European Community" for historic, organic nationalities. Here we may take a lesson from the Founding Fathers, who, confronted with a similar problem, sought a solution commensurate with the problem: "a republican remedy," as the *Federalist Papers* put it, "for the diseases most incident to republican government."

So we should be inspired to seek a nationalist remedy for the diseases most incident to nationalism—not the denial of nationalism in the name of a synthetic internationalism, but the affirmation of nationalism "rightly understood," as Tocqueville might have said: a Western-type, civic-minded nationalism, complete with checks and balances, representative government, civic liberties, the rule of law (all of which happen to be the republican remedies for the diseases of republicanism). And among these remedies (as both Tocqueville and the Founding Fathers recognized) is religion itself—or, rather, a plurality of religions, religions that tolerate one another and that are themselves not merely tolerated but respected, and not merely as a private affair but as an integral part of public life.

It is one of the bitter ironies of history that now, when the newer nationalities are becoming more aggressive and brutal, the older ones are becoming more diffident and passive, reluctant to affirm the legitimacy of their own civic, pacific mode of nationalism, let alone to impugn the legitimacy of the despotic, tribal mode that is now emerging. During the Second World War, George Orwell observed that only in England were intellectuals "ashamed of their own nationality."[24] Today that might be said of intellectuals in all the liberal democracies, who "demystify" and denigrate their own nationalities as "Eurocentric," xenophobic, even racist, while at the same time giving legitimacy to nationalities in the Third World and elsewhere which are notably illiberal, inhumane, and, not infrequently, racist.

Yet the most egregious abuses of nationalism may give us ground for hope. If we can no longer deny the reality of nationalism, we may find ourselves making the kinds of distinctions and judgments that are congruent with that reality. The bloody spectacle of nationalism at its worst, a nationalism that degrades religion as well as itself, may teach us to appreciate nationalism at its best, a nationalism tempered and elevated by religion as well as by all the other resources of civilization.

VI

Where Have All the Footnotes Gone?

A HISTORIAN BROUGHT UP in the old school of footnoting is struck by the growing number of scholarly books that have no notes at all, that even pride themselves on their lack of notes.[1] Like all moral lapses, this one started on a slippery slope: the relegation of notes to the back of the book, the conversion of footnotes to endnotes. And, like all such lapses, this one has a venerable precedent.

It was in 1755, in his *Discourse on the Origin and Foundations of Inequality Among Men* (familiarly known as the *Second Discourse*) that Jean-Jacques Rousseau appended to the preface a "Notice on the Notes":

I have added some notes to this work, following my lazy custom of working in fits and starts. These notes sometimes stray so far from the subject that they are

not good to read with the text. I have therefore relegated them to the end of the Discourse, in which I have
tried my best to follow the straightest path. Those who
have the courage to begin again will be able to amuse
themselves the second time in beating the bushes, and
try to go through the notes. There will be little harm if
others do not read them at all.[2]

Rousseau's notes have intrigued scholars who find in them
hidden meanings not available in the text, and who interpret
the "Notice" itself, professing to belittle the notes, as an
invitation to read them most carefully and seriously. (An
editor has appended a note to this note pointing out that
Rousseau elsewhere insists that his books have to be read at
least twice, which means that the notes in this book must also
be read.)[3] A more literal-minded reader, however, may take
Rousseau's directive at face value, as a justification for the
now common practice of placing notes (when there still are
notes) at the back of the book.

In extenuation of Rousseau, it should be said that his notes
are discursive and reflective rather than bibliographical or
evidential. If he has an esoteric strategy, saying one thing in
the text and another in the notes, that is the philosopher's
privilege. It is also the philosopher's privilege to be a thinker
rather than a scholar, drawing upon inner "resources,"
which are not readily documented, rather than external
"sources," which are. But historians cannot claim that dis-
pensation—or at least have not done so until recently.*

---

*To a historian of the old school, discursive footnotes (like this)
are almost as reprehensible as endnotes (like those in this book).
The old principle was that if the comment was relevant it should
appear in the text; and if it was not relevant, it should not appear
at all. It is still a good principle, certainly for the novice and proba-

In any case, with the banishment of notes to the back of the book, they have lost their honorable status as footnotes and assumed the demeaning position of endnotes. Publishers instigated this practice primarily as an economy measure to reduce the costs of typesetting. With the new mechanized and computerized processes, that is no longer a consideration. But the practice has been perpetuated for commercial reasons, to make scholarly books look more accessible and thus more marketable. And authors have acquiesced in it, hoping to attract innocent readers by hiding the scholarly paraphernalia.

In fact, so far from becoming more readable, scholarly books have become considerably less so. Nonscholarly readers have long since learned to ignore the superscripts in the text and the footnotes in small print at the bottom of the page. And scholars, who love footnotes (some prefer the footnotes to the text), and who continue to make up the bulk of the readers, are sorely inconvenienced. Instead of dropping their eyes to the bottom of the page to find the source of a quotation (and, if they are lucky, an acerbic comment by the author) and returning to the text without skipping a beat, they are now obliged to turn to the back of the book, thus interrupting their reading of the text and losing their place to boot. Indeed, they lose their place twice over, for in order to locate the endnote they have first to turn back the pages of the text to find the chapter number, which will then guide them to the page at the back of the book containing the endnotes for that chapter. Even on those too rare occasions (such as this book) where the publisher has thoughtfully provided running heads on the endnote pages indicating the corresponding pages

---

bly for all historians, and a departure from it should be understood as sheer self-indulgence.

in the text, it takes two bookmarks to keep track of one's place in the text as well as in the back of the book.

The physical discomfort of the reader is the least of the evils resulting from the displacement of footnotes. More serious is the demoralizing effect on the author. This exhibits itself initially in a cavalier attitude toward the form of citations. With the notes relegated to obscurity, the author is apt to be negligent about the proper conformation of the vital data: author (first name or initials first), title (of book italicized, of article in quotation marks), name of editor or translator (if necessary), place and date of publication (and publisher if desired, all within parentheses), volume number (in capital Roman numerals), page number (Arabic numerals).

This, however, is only the beginning of the slippery slope, for the indifference to form inevitably engenders an indifference to content. Having violated the proprieties of sequence, punctuation, and the like, the author is tempted to be careless about such details as accuracy and relevance. It is easier at the back of the book than at the bottom of the page to give a faulty or incomplete citation, or to parade one's erudition (or conceal one's ignorance) by citing a dozen sources rather than the single pertinent one. And from such peccadilloes one may soon lapse into contempt for any kind of notes and dispense with them altogether.

The gravity of this situation can be fully appreciated only by survivors of the most arduous school of footnoters: University of Chicago Ph.D.s of the 1940–60 vintage. Aging Ph.D.s from other universities, reminiscing about their graduate-school experiences, tend to be obsessed with their oral examinations, relating, with quavering voice and total recall, the cruel and unusual questions put to them by their interrogators. For University of Chicago graduates, these traumatic memories are overshadowed by the formidable figure of Kate L. Turabian.

Miss Turabian (even the most irreverent of us never spoke of her as Turabian, still less as Kate) held no professorial chair, but she had the unique and powerful position of "dissertation secretary." Outside of the university, she is remembered as the author of the much reprinted (and revised) manual for dissertations, professional journals, and books with any pretense to scholarly reputability.[4] It is her manual that laid down such arcane and inviolable rules as that the author in a footnote appears with the given name preceding the surname, while the reverse is the case in the bibliography; or that the title of a book is underlined or italicized, whereas that of an article or unpublished book is in quotation marks and neither underlined nor italicized; or that a quotation of two or more sentences *and* four or more lines is indented and single-spaced, whereas a one-sentence quotation longer than four lines or a quotation of two or more sentences shorter than four lines is neither indented nor single-spaced.

In the publishing world at large, these rules were regarded as a matter of convenience and convention. At the University of Chicago, where Miss Turabian personally enforced them and ruthlessly rejected any dissertation deviating from them, they were matters of the greatest urgency. They acquired, in fact, something of a mystique. A cynic might think them trivial and willful, the sophomoric initiation rites into academia, the dues paid to the guild in return for the privileges and perquisites of a professorship. To the true believer they were the articles of faith to which one subscribed on entering an honorable and exacting profession. Some of these articles might seem arbitrary; even a devout Anglican might jib at some of the Thirty-nine Articles, or the pious Jew at some of the 613 commandments of his faith*—which was more like the number of rules in Miss Turabian's manual style sheet. But the canon as a whole had the quality and authority of a covenant. Or, rather, it established two covenants: the first among the scholars themselves, the members of the clerisy, binding them to a common credo; the second between the clerics and the laity, the authors and their readers, serving as a pledge of orthodoxy and righteousness.

For those of a less religious turn of mind, the rules governing footnotes (that there should be footnotes went without question) were a warrant, if not of righteousness, then of accountability. And so they still are for the traditional historian. They are meant to permit the reader to check the author's sources, facts, quotations, inferences, and generalizations. This is the rationale for rules that might otherwise seem arbitrary. In prescribing the exact form and sequence of the citation, they make it not only easier for the reader to locate and check it, but also encourage the author to be more meticulous in presenting it and more responsible in drawing conclusions from it. This is why an annotated bibliography is no substitute for footnotes; it may attest to the author's erudition but does not provide the means of verification. It is also why endnotes are less satisfactory than footnotes;

---

*According to Miss Turabian, numbers with fewer than three digits should be written out, while those with three digits or more appear as numerals, except where the smaller numbers are in close proximity to the larger ones, in which case both are given as numerals. (On no occasion may a sentence start with a numeral.) In this case, "Thirty-nine Articles" is a collective and proper noun rather than a mere number, so it is exempt from this rule.

To a strict-constructionist, the placing of this footnote in the middle of a sentence is improper. In this instance, the deviation from the rule seems to me justified (although I would never have taken such liberties in the old days).

remote from the text, the citations are apt to be less precise and less pertinent.

Even the most zealous footnoter would concede that footnotes are only a partial guarantee of integrity and accountability. They make it possible to determine whether a quotation has been accurately transcribed and whether the source contains the facts attributed to it, but not whether the quotation or source is itself accurate, adequate, or relevant. They do, however, make it easier for a diligent reader to judge a quotation's accuracy, adequacy, and relevance. And they make it a little harder for authors (not impossible, authors being notably ingenious and not notably scrupulous) to distort the source or deviate too far from it. If footnotes do not quite put the fear of God into scholars, they do make them more fearful than they might otherwise be of colleagues so inconsiderate and untrusting as to check their citations and actually read their sources.

The explanations offered by historians who choose to dispense with notes (either footnotes or endnotes) are varied. Some make no mention of it at all, presumably on the principle that a gentleman (or a scholar) never explains and never apologizes. Others do explain, more or less apologetically. Several invoke the figure of the "general reader" who does not want or need notes and would only be distracted by them. It is odd to find this explanation offered in the case of a long and immensely detailed biography of Frederick the Great,[5] or of a social history of Victorian Britain full of facts and figures—and odder still to find the scholarly author of that social history speaking derisively of documentation as "a parade of attribution, exegesis, and qualification which some readers might find irritating and superfluous."[6] For the sake of the "general reader," Michael Holroyd omitted notes from his three-volume biography of George Bernard Shaw; and for the sake of the scholarly reader, he provided them in a separate volume after the completion of the entire work—at which time, years later, the readers of the earlier volumes could presumably go back and look up the references.[7] Daniel Boorstin has devised an even more inaccessible repository for the footnotes: an annotated manuscript on deposit in the Library of Congress.[8] One might think that any reader of books on these subjects of this length would not be put off by notes discreetly placed at the end of the book—and even more discreetly, as is often the case these days, without the presence of super-script numbers.

Some authors manage to inflate the scholarly character of their works while justifying the absence of scholarly materials. One explains that his sources are so vast that to cite all of them is "impractical"[9]; another that his sources are largely in foreign languages and in places too remote or recondite for readers in the United States.[10] Still others demean the conventions of scholarship while professing a more exalted sense of the historical calling—and a more exalted sense of themselves as scholars beyond reproach and beyond the need to establish their credentials by such petty means as the citation of sources. Arno Mayer, having written a highly controversial and totally undocumented book on the Holocaust, told an interviewer that footnotes are "a fetish [that] very often interferes with careful intellection and rumination."[11] Another revisionist historian, William Appleman Williams, finds footnotes or bibliographies "poor jokes" for a book of "this nature," since the source of any quotation is meaningless except in relation to all the other documents and to the author's "process of reflection." If the reader trusts the author because the source of the quotation is cited, Williams sees no reason why the reader should distrust him because it is not. "History," he loftily concludes, "is simply not the arithmetic total of footnotes."[12] This argument, that the historian need not prove himself to the reader, takes on a special meaning in the context of "multiculturalism." The coauthors of a book on Native Americans find the very idea of footnotes demeaning: "It is our culture and history and we do not have to prove it to anyone by footnoting."[13]*

So far, most historians have resisted these ostensibly high-minded, and self-serving, reasons for dispensing with notes. They may make their obeisance to the idols of the market-place, acquiescing in endnotes rather than footnotes, and departing, on occasion, from the strict regimen of Miss Turabian. But they observe the principles and practices of documentation, out of respect as much for their readers as for the conventions of their craft.

God, it has been said, resides in the details. (A corrupt version, which I hotly reject, has the Devil residing in the details.) I hope it is not sacrilegious to suggest that scholarship too resides in the detail. The footnote would seem to be the smallest detail in a work of history. Yet it carries a large burden of responsibility, testifying to the validity of the work, to the integrity (and the humility) of the historian, and to the dignity of the discipline.

---

*After such belittling remarks by professional historians, it is interesting to read of the experience of Alan Watkins, an English journalist with an old-fashioned respect for history, who took the trouble to document his book on Margaret Thatcher, only to be told by some reviewers that the footnotes were "irritating" and "pedantic."[14]

VII

Postmodernist History

FOR THE HISTORIAN, as for the philosopher, the quarrel between the Ancients and the Moderns is being superseded by a quarrel between the Moderns and the Postmoderns. If the great subversive principle of modernity is historicism—a form of relativism that locates the meaning of ideas and events so firmly in their historical context that history, rather than philosophy and nature, becomes the arbiter of truth—postmodernism is now confronting us with a far more subversive form of relativism, a relativism so radical, so absolute, as to be antithetical to both history and truth.* For postmodernism denies not only suprahistorical truths but historical truths, truths relative to particular times and places. And that denial involves a repudiation of the

---

* "History," in this context, refers to writings about the past rather than the past itself.

historical enterprise as it has been understood and practiced until very recently.

Postmodernism (or poststructuralism—the terms are by now used interchangeably—or "pomo," as it is familiarly called in academic circles and computer networks) is best known as a school of literary theory. But it is becoming increasingly prominent in such other disciplines as history, philosophy, anthropology, law, and theology (and in architecture, where it has a more specialized meaning). Its forefathers are Nietzsche and Heidegger, its fathers Derrida and Foucault; that the latter have vigorously disputed each other does not diminish the enthusiasm of disciples who find them equally congenial and compatible. From Jacques Derrida postmodernism has borrowed the vocabulary and basic concepts of "deconstruction": the "aporia" of discourse, the indeterminacy and contrariness of language, the "fictive" and "duplicitous" nature of signs and symbols, the dissociation of words from any presumed reality. From Michel Foucault it has adopted the idea of power: the "power structure" immanent not only in language—the words and ideas that "privilege" the "hegemonic" groups in society—but in the very nature of knowledge, which is itself an instrument and product of power. The combined effect of these doctrines is to impugn traditional rational discourse as "logocentric," "phallocentric," "totalizing," "authoritarian."*

---

*This description of postmodernism by a postmodernist may read like a parody, but it is all too typical of the genre:

> . . . indeterminacy and immanence; ubiquitous simulacra, pseudo-events; a conscious lack of mastery, lightness and evanescence everywhere; a new temporality, or rather intemporality, a polychronic sense of history; a patchwork or ludic, transgressive or deconstructive approach to knowledge and authority; an ironic, parodic, reflexive, fantastic awareness of the moment; a linguistic turn, semiotic imperative in culture;

In literature, postmodernism amounts to a denial of the fixity of any "text," of the authority of the author over the interpreter, of any "canon" that privileges great books over lesser ones. In philosophy, it is a denial of the fixity of language, of any correspondence between language and reality—indeed, of any "essential" reality and thus of any proximate truth about reality. In law (in America, at any rate), it is a denial of the fixity of the Constitution, of the authority of the founders of the Constitution, and of the legitimacy of law itself, which is regarded as nothing more than an instrument of power. In history, it is a denial of the fixity of the past, of the reality of the past apart from what the historian chooses to make of it, and thus of any objective truth about the past.

Postmodernist history, one might say, recognizes no reality principle, only the pleasure principle—history at the pleasure of the historian. To appreciate its full import, one should see it in the perspective of what might be called "modernist" history, now generally known as "traditional" history.

Modernist history is not positivist, in the sense of aspiring to a fixed, total, or absolute truth about the past. Like postmodernist history, it is relativistic, but with a difference, for its relativism is firmly rooted in reality. It is skeptical of absolute truth but not of partial, contingent, incremental truths. More important, it does not deny the reality of the past itself. Like the political philosopher who makes it a principle to read the works of the Ancients in the spirit of the Ancients, so the modernist historian reads and writes history in that spirit, with a scrupulous regard for the histo-

---

and in society generally the violence of local desires diffused into a terminology of seduction and force.[1]

ricity, the integrity, the actuality of the past. He makes a strenuous effort to enter into the minds and experiences of people in the past, to try to understand them as they understood themselves, to rely upon contemporary evidence as much as possible, to intrude his own views and assumptions as little as possible, to reconstruct to the best of his ability the past as it "actually was," in Leopold von Ranke's celebrated and now much derided phrase.

Like modernist literature and art, modernist history is an exacting discipline, requiring a great exercise of self-restraint, even self-sacrifice. The greatest of modernist poets, T. S. Eliot, once said, "The progress of an artist is a continual self-sacrifice, a continual extinction of personality."[2] And so it is with the historian, who strives constantly to transcend his own present in order to recapture the past, to suppress his own personality in order to give life to generations long dead. This self-sacrifice is all the greater because the historian is well aware that his effort will never entirely succeed, that the past will always, to some degree, elude him.

Historians, ancient and modern, have always known what postmodernism professes to have just discovered—that any work of history is vulnerable on three counts: the fallibility and deficiency of the historical record on which it is based; the fallibility and selectivity inherent in the writing of history; and the fallibility and subjectivity of the historian. As long as historians have reflected upon their craft, they have known that the past cannot be recaptured in its entirety, if only because the remains of the past are incomplete and are themselves part of the present, so that the past itself is, in this sense, irredeemably present. They have also known that the writing of history necessarily entails selection and interpretation, that there is inevitable distortion in the very attempt to present a coherent account of an often inchoate past, that, therefore, every historical work is necessarily imperfect, tentative, and partial (in both senses of the word).

Historians have also known—they would have to be extraordinarily obtuse not to—that they themselves live and act and think in their own present, that some of the assumptions they bring to history derive from, and are peculiar to, their own culture, that others may reflect the particular race, gender, and class to which they belong, and that still others emanate from ideas and beliefs that are unique to themselves as individuals. It did not take Carl Becker, in 1931, to discover that "Everyman [is] his own historian";[3] or Charles Beard, in 1934, to reveal that "each historian who writes history is the product of his age."[4] Beard pointed out that these propositions had been familiar "for a century or more"—thus antedating even Marx. Forty years before Beard delivered his famous presidential address to the American Historical Association, William Sloane, professor of history at Columbia University, inaugurated the first issue of the *American Historical Review* with a lead article announcing: "History will not stay written. Every age demands a history written from its own standpoint—with reference to its own social conditions, its thought, its beliefs and its acquisitions—and thus comprehensible to the men who live in it."[5]

It is useful for historians to be reminded of what they have always known—the frailty, fallibility, and relativity of the historical enterprise—if only to realize that these ideas are not the great discoveries of postmodernism. Yet in their familiar form, they are very different from the tidings brought by postmodernism. For the presumption of postmodernism is that all of history is fatally flawed, and that because there is no absolute, total truth, there can be no partial, contingent truths. More important still is the presumption that because it is impossible to attain such truths, it is not only futile but positively baneful to aspire to them.

. . .

In a sense, modernism anticipated and tried to forestall the absolutistic relativism of postmodernism by creating a "discipline" of history. Conscious of the deficiencies both of the historian and of the historical record, acutely aware of the ambiguous relationship between past and present, the profession created a discipline of checks and controls designed to compensate for those deficiencies. This is the meaning of the historical revolution that drew upon such diverse sources as Enlightenment rationalism, Germanic scholarship, and academic professionalism to produce what was once called "critical history."*

Critical history puts a premium on archival research and primary sources, the authenticity of documents and reliability of witnesses, the need to obtain substantiating and countervailing evidence; and, at a more mundane level, the accuracy of quotations and citations, prescribed forms of documentation in footnotes and bibliography, and all the rest of the "methodology" that goes into the "canon of evidence." The purpose of this methodology is twofold: to bring to the surface the infrastructure, as it were, of the historical work, thus making it accessible to the reader and exposing it to criticism; and to encourage the historian to a maximum exertion of objectivity in spite of all the temptations to the contrary. Postmodernists scoff at this aim as the

---

*This is very different from Nietzsche's sense of "critical" history— a history in the "service of life," in contrast to "monumental" history, which celebrates a mythical past, and "antiquarian" history, which is pure pedantry. It is also different from the recent usage of "critical," as in "critical legal theory," which is a cross between deconstruction and Marxism. The original sense of "critical history" is exactly the opposite—an attempt to be as rigorous, accurate, objective, and scholarly as possible.

antiquated remnant of nineteenth-century positivism. But it has been the norm of the profession until recently. "No one," the American historian John Higham wrote, "including the 'literary' historians, rejected the ideal of objectivity in the ordinary sense of unbiased truth; no one gave up the effort to attain it; and no one thought it wholly unapproachable."[6] This was in 1965, well after Becker and Beard had "relativized" history but before Foucault and Derrida had "postmodernized" it.

Here lies the crucial distinction between modernism and postmodernism, between the old relativistic relativism, one might say, and the new absolutistic version. Where modernism tolerates relativism, postmodernism celebrates it. Where modernism, aware of the obstacles in the way of objectivity, regards this as a challenge and makes a strenuous effort to attain as much objectivity and unbiased truth as possible, postmodernism takes the rejection of absolute truth as a deliverance from all truth and from the obligation to maintain any degree of objectivity.

From the postmodernist perspective, modernist history is as uncritical as the history it professes to transcend—as mythical and honorific as Nietzsche's "monumental" history. And it is all the more spurious because it conceals its ideological structure behind a scholarly façade of footnotes and "facts" (in quotation marks, in the postmodernist lexicon). To "demythicize" or "demystify" this history, postmodernism has to expose not only its ideology—the hegemonic, privileged, patriarchal interests served by this history—but also its methodology, the scholarly apparatus that gives it a specious credibility. This is the twofold agenda of postmodernism: to free history from the shackles of an authoritarian ideology, and to release it from the constraints of a delusive methodology. The ultimate aim is even more ambitious: to liberate us all from the coercive ideas of truth and reality.

This is not the familiar kind of historical revisionism that revises or reinterprets a particular account of a particular event or period. It goes well beyond that, for it is profoundly skeptical, even cynical, about all of traditional history—its assumptions and intentions, methods and conclusions. It is not so much a revision of modernist history as a repudiation of it.

Theodore Zeldin was one of the first historians (as distinct from philosophers of history) to launch a serious, sustained assault upon modernist history. That history, he claimed—traditional narrative history—is dependent upon such "tyrannical" concepts as causality, chronology, and collectivity (the latter including class as well as nationality). To liberate history from these constraints, he proposed a new history on the model of a *pointilliste* painting, composed entirely of unconnected dots. This would have the double advantage of emancipating the historian from the tyrannies of the discipline, and emancipating the reader from the tyranny of the historian, since the reader would be free to make "what lines he thinks fit for himself."[7]* More recently, Zeldin has gone so far by way of liberation as to liberate himself from history itself, this time by invoking a literary model. "Free history," he now finds, can only take the form of fiction[9]––in testimony to which he has written a novel entitled *Happiness*.

Not all postmodernists go as far as Zeldin in seeking that ultimate liberation from history, but all share his aversion to the conventions and categories of traditional history.

---

*An art historian finds the same "democratizing purpose" in the original *pointilliste*, Georges Seurat, who is said to have tried to create an art that would be "a sort of democratically oriented, high-type painting-by-dots which would totally wipe out the role of genius, the exceptional creative figure, in the making of art, even 'great art.' "[8]

Following Derrida's strictures against "chronophonism," Dominick LaCapra has deconstructed historical chronology, explaining that even so simple a fact as the date of an event depends on "what is for some historians a belief and for others a convenient fiction: the decisive significance of the birth of Christ in establishing a chronology in terms of a 'before' and 'after.' "[10]* A less sophisticated historian might observe that the issue is not what some historians happen to believe but what contemporaries at the time believed. But the postmodernist, being as skeptical of the authority of contemporaries as of all other authorities, is unpersuaded by so prosaic an argument.

Narrative history—"narrativity," as the postmodernist says—is the primary culprit, not only because it depends upon such arbitrary conventions as chronology, causality, and collectivity, but also because it takes the form of a logical, orderly structure of discourse that is presumed to correspond, at least in some measure, to the reality of the past, and thus communicates, again in some measure, a truth about the past. This is the illusion that the postmodernist seeks to expose: that the narratives of history are anything more than the rhetorical, literary, aesthetic creations of the historian.

The "aestheticization" of history is most evident in the work of the leading postmodernist philosopher of history, Hayden White. To the traditional historian, this kind of philosophy of history appears to be more philosophical than historical and more literary than philosophical. Thus, one

---

*By this reasoning, a Jewish historian would be justified in giving the date of the fall of the Bastille as the 20th of Tammuz 5549—which is accurate but, the traditional historian would say, irrelevant and profoundly unhistorical.

of White's essays is titled "The Historical Text as Literary Artifact,"[11] and one of the chapters in his most influential work, *Metahistory*, is called "The Poetics of History." The preface to *Metahistory* explains that each of the subjects, from Hegel to Benedetto Croce, represents a particular aspect of the "historical imagination": metaphor, metonymy, synecdoche, and irony.[12]*

For White, as for postmodernists generally, there is no distinction between history and philosophy or between history and literature—or between history and "antihistory," which is why he can describe the pyschoanalytic study *Life Against Death* as a brilliant work of "antihistory," and then insist that its author, Norman O. Brown, is surely worthy of consideration as a "serious historian").[13] All of history, in this view, is aesthetic and philosophical, its only meaning or "reality" (again, in quotation marks) being that which the historian chooses to give it in accord with his own sensibility and disposition. What the traditional historian sees as an event that actually occurred in the past, the postmodernist sees as a "text" that exists only in the present—a text to be parsed, glossed, construed, and interpreted by the historian, much as a poem or novel is by the critic. And, like any literary text, the historical text is indeterminate and contradictory, paradoxical and ironic, rhetorical and metaphoric.

In postmodernist history, as in postmodernist literary criticism, theory has become a calling in itself. Just as there are professors of literature who never engage in the actual interpretation of literary works—and even disdain interpretation as an inferior vocation—so there are professors of

---

*White did not coin the term "metahistory," but he gave it its present connotation and is responsible for its widespread usage. It had earlier been used in the sense of mythical history rather than the philosophy or theory of history.

history who have never (at least to judge by their published work) done research in or written about an actual historical event or period. Their professional careers are devoted to speculation about the theory or philosophy of history—"metahistory"—and to the active promotion of some particular methodology or ideology of history.

But it is not only metahistorians who reject such naïve notions as reality and truth. More and more practicing historians are beginning to share that attitude, almost unwittingly, reflexively. An essay in a recent issue of the *American Historical Review* casually observes that while "contemporary historians seldom believe anymore that they can or should try to capture 'the truth,' " this does not absolve them from passing judgment on their subjects. In support of this proposition, the author cites an earlier president of the American Historical Association, Gordon Wright, who had given it as his credo that "our search for truth ought to be quite consciously suffused by a commitment to some deeply held humane values."[14] The quotation actually speaks against the thesis of this article, for Wright made that commitment to humane values as part of "our search for truth." But that was in 1975, when it was still possible to speak respectfully of the search for truth—and, indeed, to speak of truth without the ironic use of quotation marks.

The disdain for truth, not only as an ultimate philosophical principle but as a practical, guiding rule of historical scholarship, is dramatically illustrated by the controversy over a book on the Weimar Republic by David Abraham. The book was criticized by some eminent historians for being full of errors—misquotations, faulty citations, unwarranted deductions from the sources—and was defended by an equally eminent group of historians who rallied to the side of the author.[15] The first line of defense was to impugn the political and personal motives of the critics, suggesting that they were really objecting to the Marxist thesis of the book rather than to its faulty scholarship, and that they were resentful of a novice who dared infringe on their turf.[16] The second line of defense was to belittle the seriousness of the errors and the standards of scholarship by which so much was made of them. One historian described the mistakes as innocent faults of transcription such as occur in any archival research and are typical of the "general messiness of life."[17] Another said that the errors, however "glaring and inexcusable," did not affect the "historical configuration" or "interpretive logic" of the book.[18]

In an article entitled " 'Facts' and History," Thomas Bender turned the argument against Abraham's critics, chastising them for being so naïve as to believe in "the absolute certitude of historical fact." To be sure, he conceded, documents should be "accurately transcribed and properly cited." But the real issue in this case, as he saw it, was the nature of the "historical imagination," and this involves a process of "imaginative creation" that goes well beyond documents and facts. "Young historians," Bender concluded, "will never learn their craft if their elders become fact fetishists."[19]*

Hard cases, it is said, make bad law. History, however, all too often consists of hard cases, and historical methods are designed to accommodate them. For all historians, traditional and "new" alike, the hardest case in modern history is surely the Holocaust. It is especially hard for postmodernists, who face the prospect of doing to the Holocaust what they do to all of history—relativizing, problematizing, ulti-

---

*Henry Turner, Abraham's main critic, anticipated that he himself would be accused of being a "vulgar factologist."[20]

mately aestheticizing or fictionalizing it. One postmodernist historian, Jane Caplan, raises the problem, only to confess that she cannot resolve it.

> To put it bluntly, what can one usefully say about National Socialism as an ideology or a political movement and regime via theories that appear to discount rationality as a mode of explanation, that resist the claims of truth, relativize and disseminate power, cannot assign responsibility clearly, and do not privilege (one) truth or morality over (multiple) interpretation? . . . It is one thing to embrace poststructuralism and postmodernism, to disseminate power, to decenter subjects, and all in all let a hundred kinds of meaning contend, when *Bleak House* or philology or even the archaeology of knowledge are the issue. But should the rules of contention be different when it is a question, not simply of History, but of a recent history of lives, deaths, and suffering, and the concept of a justice that seeks to draw some meaningful relation between these?[21]

The difficulty is compounded by the existence of a school of thought that relativizes, "deprivileges," "decenters," indeed, deconstructs the Holocaust so thoroughly as to deny its reality. It is this "revisionist" thesis that postmodernists would like to avoid. But they can do so only by the kind of verbal legerdemain that is their stock-in-trade—and that has created the problem in the first place.

Hayden White poses the dilemma and attempts to solve it. If all historical narratives ("modes of emplotment," in the postmodernist vocabulary) are rhetorical devices, if no one mode can be judged to be more "true" to the "facts" than any other because there are no "facts" from which one may elicit "truths," is there any basis on which to choose among the alternative modes? Can one say, for example, that the comic or pastoral modes are "unacceptable" as "representations" of the Holocaust? Are there any "limits" on the kinds of stories that can "responsibly" be told about the Holocaust? There could be such limits, White reasons, only if one believes that the events themselves possess some inherent "meaning," so that there is some correspondence between the "facts" and the mode of emplotment. But since that is not the case, since the comic and pastoral modes, like any others, are "figurative" rather than "literal," White concludes that there are no limits to the kinds of stories the historian might choose to tell and no grounds on which to reject one or another mode.[22]

Indeed, the comic mode, White points out, has been effectively used in a comic-book version of the Holocaust, in which the Germans are portrayed as cats, the Jews as mice, and the Poles as pigs. *Maus* is a story within a story: the author is trying to extract from his father the story of his parents' experiences as well as that of the Holocaust itself. And both stories are ironic, with all the characters—not only the "perpetrators, victims, and bystanders," but the father and son as well—resembling beasts, White says, rather than human beings. White himself finds this comic-book version of the Holocaust "one of the most moving narrative accounts" he knows, "not least because it makes the difficulty of discovering and telling the whole truth about even a small part of it as much a part of the story as the events whose meaning it is seeking to discover."[23]

It is typical of the postmodernist to find this account of the Holocaust so moving, "not least" because it makes of the Holocaust as much a metahistorical problem as a historical event—and to be moved, as well, by this ironic (and even-handed) treatment of the subject, in which everyone looks like a beast. The comic-ironic mode is congenial to the postmodernist because it has the double effect of converting history into metahistory, thus distancing the historian from anything that might resemble truth or reality, and of dehumanizing the subjects of history, thus transforming history from a humanistic discipline into a critique of humanism.

Yet White is eager to differentiate himself from the "revisionist" historian who, in a more simple-minded and less ironic fashion, denies the truth and reality of the Holocaust. He finds the solution to his dilemma in Derrida's concept of the "middle voice." It is this middle voice, neither passive nor active, that can express "something like the relationship to that event," something like the "reality" of the Holocaust, without falling into the fallacy of "realism." And not only the reality of the Holocaust but the entire "new form of historical reality," including "total war, nuclear contamination, mass starvation, and ecological suicide."[24]

This attempt to deconstruct (White never uses the term) the Holocaust without denying it, to affirm something like a "reality" that is not a reality, to make the Holocaust "unique" and at the same time part of a larger phenomenon—all of this, obviously, raises many problems. The historian Martin Jay (himself more of a Marxist or historicist than a deconstructionist) takes White to task for compromising his principles: "In his anxiety to avoid inclusion in the ranks of those who argue for a kind of relativistic 'anything goes,' which might provide ammunition for revisionist skeptics about the existence of the Holocaust, he undercuts what is most powerful in his celebrated critique of naïve historical realism."[25] Carlo Ginzburg (whose work superficially resembles that of the postmodernist), is distressed not by White's abandoning his principles but by his remaining true to them. He quotes a moving passage from a letter by Pierre Vidal-Naquet, whose mother died at Auschwitz and who had earlier written an essay refuting the arch-revisionist Robert Faurisson. The *affaire Faurisson*, Vidal-Naquet says, convinced him that the old Rankean notion of reality cannot be dismissed and that there is "something irreducible" that, for better or worse, can only be called "reality." "Without this reality," he asks, "how could we make a difference between fiction and history?"[26]

If in the hard case of the Holocaust postmodernism finds it difficult to sustain the "difference between fiction and history," it has less reason to try to do so in the case of less sensitive subjects. Committed to the "fictive" nature of history, liberated from "fact fetishism," uninhibited and unapologetic in the exercise of the "imaginative creation" that is presumed to be of the essence of the "historical imagination," postmodernist history may well take the form of fictional history.

This new kind of fictional history is very different from the familiar genre of historical fiction. The historical novel, as it has evolved from Walter Scott to the flourishing industry that it is today, has never been a challenge to traditional history because it has been understood as a distinctive form of fiction, not of history—as historical fiction, not fictional history. Only when history itself is "problematized" and "deconstructed," when events and persons are transformed into "texts," when the past is deprived of any reality and history of any truth, does the distinction between history and fiction become blurred or elided. It is then that fictional history becomes a form of history rather than fiction, and that history itself may be seen as "historiographic metafiction."[27]*

Many historians who shy away from any suggestion of fictional or even "metafictional" history welcome the invitation to be "imaginative," "inventive," "creative"—words

---

*By the same token, biography is said to have embraced a "new methodology," a " 'freedom' from fact," that makes it "ultimately fiction."[28]

bandied about so frequently in the profession today that one almost does not notice them or consider their implication. Yet they have contributed to the "widespread tendency," as the late Arnaldo Momigliano observed, to treat history as "another genre of fiction."[29] Where once historians were exhorted to be accurate and factual, they are now urged to be imaginative and inventive. Instead of "re-creating" the past, they are told to "create" it; instead of "reconstructing" history, to "construct" or "deconstruct" it. A recent French study of Richelieu asks, only partly tongue-in-cheek, "Did Richelieu—Armand Jean du Plessis—exist? Didn't the narratives invent him?"[30]

Formerly, when historians invoked the idea of imagination, they meant the exercise of imagination required to transcend the present and immerse oneself in the past. This is the genius attributed to the great nineteenth-century historians: "empathy, imagination, the attempt to place oneself in an historic situation and into an historic character without prejudgment."[31] For the postmodernist it means exactly the opposite: the imagination to create a past in the image of the present and in accord with the prejudgment of the present-minded historian.

History, Macaulay said, is a "debatable land" governed by two hostile powers, Reason and Imagination, falling "alternately under the sole and absolute dominion of each." But he then went on to place significant limits on the dominion of the imagination.

> A perfect historian must possess an imagination sufficiently powerful to make his narrative affecting and picturesque. Yet he must control it so absolutely as to content himself with the materials which he finds, and to refrain from supplying deficiencies by additions of his own. He must be a profound and ingenious rea-

soner. Yet he must possess sufficient self-command to abstain from casting his facts in the mould of his hypothesis.[32]

Later in the essay Macaulay described the "art of historical narration" as the ability to affect the reader's imagination "without indulging in the licence of invention." And he compared the historian to the dramatist, "with one obvious distinction": "The dramatist creates: the historian only disposes."[33]

Even Macaulay's great-nephew G. M. Trevelyan, the most "literary" of historians, put the imagination under strict constraints:

> The appeal of history to us all is in the last analysis poetic. But the poetry of history does not consist of imagination roaming at large, but of imagination pursuing the fact and fastening upon it. That which compels the historian to 'scorn delights and live laborious days' is the ardour of his own curiosity to know what really happened long ago in that land of mystery which we call the past.[34]

If postmodernism appeals to the creative imagination of the historian, it also appeals to the political imagination. Yet its political implications, like much else about it, are ambiguous. Some radicals criticize it for being so unremitting and negative in its rejection of modernity that it provides no grounds for resistance. "Since it commits you to affirming nothing," says Terry Eagleton (a Marxist and "New Historicist"), "it is as injurious as blank ammunition."[35] Jürgen Habermas goes so far as to call Foucault and Derrida "Young Conservatives" because of their "de-centered subjectivity" and "irreconcilable anti-modernism."[36] The social critic (and social democrat) Michael Walzer criticizes Foucault for not being a "good revolutionary," because Foucault does not believe in the reality of the state or ruling class and therefore cannot believe in the overthrow of the state and of the ruling class; neither is he a good reformer, because he has no "regulative principles with which we might set things right."[37]

Other commentators emphasize the radical and subversive effect of postmodernism in general and of the ideas of Foucault and Derrida in particular. One of Foucault's admirers sees him as "continuing the work of the Western Marxists by other means";[38] and another describes his "radical reformism" not as a form of passivity but as a "tactical hyper-activism."[39] Peter Stearns (editor of the *Journal of Social History*) finds in postmodernism the support for non-Marxist forms of radicalism, such as the "currently-fashionable protest ideologies of the academic world"—anti-racism, anti-sexism, environmentalism. "Postmodernists," he observes, "are clearly spurred by a desire to find new intellectual bases for radicalism, given the troubles of liberalism and socialism."[40] Eagleton, having criticized postmodernism for being negative and passive, makes a point of exempting Derrida from these strictures. "Derrida is clearly out to do more than develop new techniques of reading: deconstruction is for him an ultimately *political* practice, an attempt to dismantle the logic by which a particular system of thought, and behind that a whole system of political structures and social institutions, maintains its force."[41]

Postmodernism, as Eagleton suggests, is far more radical than either Marxism or the new modish radical causes, if only because it denies the Enlightenment principles to which they are committed: reason, truth, justice, morality, reality.[42] And in denying the rhetoric and the values of the Enlightenment, it subverts the society and polity that invoke that rhetoric and those values. Thus, in rejecting the "discipline" of knowledge and rationality, postmodernism also rejects the "discipline" of social and political authority. This is the clear implication of Foucault's "Power / Knowledge" thesis, in which knowledge, the "regime of truth," is identified with the political regime of domination and oppression.[43] And it is as clearly implied in Derrida's critique of the modernist tradition—in his description, for example, of "organized narration" as "a matter for the police," a "force of order or law."[44]

The political implications of Hayden White's "metahistory" are no less obvious, although it displays a confusing (but not untypical) combination of deconstruction and Marxism. The Marxism is most conspicuous in his interpretation of traditional history as a reflection of the class interests of the bourgeoisie. His essay on the German historian Johann Droysen, subtitled "Historical Writing as a Bourgeois Science," describes history (and not only Droysen's history) "as part and parcel of the cultural superstructure of an age, as an activity that is more determined by than determinative of social praxis."[45] Another essay, "The Politics of Historical Interpretation," explains the function of the "discipline" of history: "We do not have to impute dark ideological motives to those who endowed history with the authority of a discipline in order to recognize the ideological benefits to new social classes and political constituencies that professional, academic historiography served and, *mutatis mutandis*, continues to serve down to our own time."[46]

Provoked by the charge that his own form of relativism promotes "the kind of nihilism that invites revolutionary activism of a particularly irresponsible sort," White protests that he is against revolutions, "whether launched from 'above' or 'below' in the social hierarchy." His relativism, he says, is a counsel of tolerance rather than license. Besides, in advanced countries revolution is likely to result in the consolidation of oppressive powers, since those who control the "military-industrial-economic complex hold all the cards." Instead of a political revolution of the traditional kind, he proposes, in effect, a meta-revolution, which would replace the "bourgeois ideology of realism," typified by the conventional "discipline" of history, by a view of the past as a spectacle of "confusion," "uncertainty," and "moral anarchy." Only such a "utopian," "eschatological" idea of history, he argues, is consistent with "the kind of politics that is based on a vision of a perfected society."[47]

In the familiar vocabulary of postmodernism, this anarchic, "utopian" view of history is translated as "indeterminacy." And indeterminacy is inherently radical insofar as it is a standing invitation to *creatio ex nihilo*. Having discredited the "bourgeois" discipline of history, having deconstructed both the "texts" of the past and the "texts" of all previous histories, the historian finds himself with a tabula rasa on which he may inscribe whatever past he likes. Thus the principle of indeterminacy lends itself, paradoxically, to any determinacy at all—to any part or the whole of the race / class / gender trinity, for example. By the same token, it lends itself to any kind of radical ideology the historian may choose to impose on history. (But not to any kind of conservative ideology, which implies a respect for tradition and the givens of the past, and rejects the very idea of a tabula rasa.)

The radical potential of postmodernism has been seized most enthusiastically by feminist historians, who find the old Marxism and even some forms of the new radicalism unresponsive to their concerns. It is no accident (as a Marxist would say) that so many postmodernist historians are feminists, and that postmodernism figures so prominently in feminist history. Joan Wallach Scott explains the political affinity between the two:

A more radical feminist politics (and a more radical feminist history) seems to me to require a more radical epistemology. Precisely because it addresses questions of epistemology, relativizes the status of all knowledge, links knowledge and power, and theorizes these in terms of the operations of difference, I think poststructuralism (or at least some of the approaches generally associated with Michel Foucault and Jacques Derrida) can offer feminism a powerful analytic perspective.[48]

Feminist history is consciously and implacably opposed not only to traditional history but to earlier varieties of women's history. It belittles the kind of women's history that focuses on the experiences of women in particular events and periods. It even rejects the idea of "mainstreaming" women's history into general history—the "add-women-and-stir recipe," as it is now called.[49] The new feminist history, unlike the old women's history, calls for the rewriting and "reconceptualizing" of all of history from a "consciously feminist stance" and "feminist perspective," so that it may be "seen through the eyes of women and ordered by values they define"[50]—the eyes and values of the feminist historian rather than of the women who are the ostensible subjects of history. And these values, many feminists believe, are inimical not only to the substance of traditional (and traditional women's) history, but to its methodology and mode of discourse: the logic, reason, and coherence that are themselves expressive of a patriarchal ideology.

It is this repudiation of traditional history that makes postmodernism so congenial to the feminist, and that makes its "radical epistemology," as Joan Scott says, conducive to a radical feminist politics.* Just as traditional history is an

---

*Yet even this radical epistemology is not always radical enough. It is an embarrassment to feminists, for example, that Foucault,

instrument for patriarchal power, so feminist history is an instrument for feminist power. Some feminists are more candid than others in discussing their political agenda. "We are all engaged," the authors of one essay explain, "in writing a kind of propaganda. Our stories are inspired by what could be called a world view, but what we would call politics." Since there is no objective basis for one story rather than another, the only grounds for judging one better than another are "its persuasiveness, its political utility, and its political sincerity." But the political rationale of feminist history is itself a problem, these feminists point out, for political utility might be best served by concealing or denying the theory upon which this history is based. To "problematize the past, reality, and the truth," as a properly feminist history should, is to write a history that is difficult to read and, therefore, politically inexpedient. It would surely be more persuasive if such a history assumed the "mantle of objectivity" and "mythologized" its own interpretation by presenting it as true. The authors of this essay sympathize with those feminists who resort to this stratagem, but they themselves resist it. A truly radical history, they believe, requires nothing less than a totally demythicized history.[53]

Thus it is that the "poetics" of history becomes the "politics" of history. Postmodernism, even more overtly than Marxism, makes of history—the writing of history as much as the "praxis" of history—an instrument in the struggle for power. The new historian, like the proletariat of old, is the

---

having exposed the fallacy of "sexual essentialism," persists in using traditional masculine language and rarely cites works by women.[51] One commentator (a man, as it happens) apologizes for retaining in his translations Foucault's "relentlessly masculine forms" of pronouns, and his use of "*homme*" to mean "humanity."[52]

bearer of the class / race / gender "war"—or, rather, "wars." And here lies another quandary.

What is sauce for the goose . . . If the feminist historian can and should write history from her perspective and for her political purposes, why should the black historian not do the same—even if such a history might "marginalize" women? And why not the working-class historian, who might marginalize both women and blacks? (Feminists have criticized E. P. Thompson and other radical historians on just this ground.) And why not the homosexual historian, who might marginalize heterosexuals? For that matter, why not the traditional dead-white-male (or even live-white-male) historian, who might marginalize (who has, in fact, been accused of marginalizing) all other species?

If "Everyman his own historian" must now be rendered "Everyman / woman his / her own historian"—or, as some feminists would have it, "Everywomyn her own herstorian"—why not "Every black / white / Hispanic / Asian / Native American . . ."? Or "Every Christian / Jew / Catholic / Protestant / Muslim / Hindu / agnostic / atheist . . ."? Or "Every heterosexual / homosexual / bisexual / androgynous / polymorphous / misogynous . . ."? And so on, through all the ethnic, racial, religious, sexual, national, ideological, and other characteristics that distinguish people. This sounds like a reductio ad absurdum, but it is little more than is already being affirmed in the name of "multiculturalism."

Multiculturalism has the obvious effect of politicizing history. But its more pernicious effect is to demean and dehumanize the people who are the subjects of history. To pluralize and particularize history to the point where people have no history in common is to deny the common humanity of all people, whatever their sex, race, class, religion. It is also to trivialize history by so fragmenting it that it lacks all coherence and focus, all sense of continuity—indeed, all meaning.[54]

From a postmodernist perspective, this is all to the good, for it destroys the "totalizing," "universalizing," "logocentric," "phallocentric" history that is said to be the great evil of modernity. Postmodernist history, like postmodernist literary theory, celebrates "aporia"—difference, discontinuity, disparity, contradiction, discord, ambiguity, irony, paradox, perversity, opacity, obscurity, anarchy, chaos. "We require a history," Hayden White explains, "that will educate us to discontinuity more than ever before; for discontinuity, disruption, and chaos is our lot."[55] The modernist accuses the postmodernist of bringing mankind to the abyss of nihilism. The postmodernist proudly, happily accepts that charge.

It may be said that postmodernist history is of little importance in the profession at large, that it is confined to a self-described "vanguard" that has few disciples in theory and fewer still in practice. In sheer numbers, this may be the case, although it is difficult to make such a quantitative calculation. But the question of influence is not determined by numbers, as anyone who has followed the fortunes of Marxism in the academy and in the culture at large is aware; Marxism in the 1930s was far more influential than the number of avowed Marxists would suggest. And so it is with any intellectual or cultural movement. The word "vanguard" itself is deceptive. In its original military meaning, it referred to the advance troops of the army, and the efficacy of the vanguard was assumed to depend on the size and strength of the troops behind it. In its present cultural sense, a vanguard may exist and thrive, and profoundly affect social and cultural values, without any army—with "fellow travelers" in place of troops. It is a long time since anyone has been foolish enough to ask, "How many divisions has the Pope?"

Postmodernism is less prevalent among historians than among literary critics, although there are some who regard it, even in history, as "the orthodoxy of today."[56] But if it is not quite the dominant orthodoxy, it does exercise a disproportionate influence in the profession, because it tends to attract so many of the best and the brightest, especially among the young. How can bright, ambitious young historians resist the new, especially when it has the sanction of some of their most distinguished elders? How can they resist the appeal to be on the "cutting edge" of their profession, when it carries with it not only the promise of advancement but the allure of creativity, imagination, inventiveness? And not only creativity but liberation from the tedium and rigor of the old "discipline" of history?

This last is a matter of more than passing importance, in explaining both the attraction of postmodernist history and its influence. Postmodernism, even more than the older varieties of the new history, makes obsolete any course on methodology, because any prescribed methodology is regarded as arbitrary and "privileged." The absence of such a course, the lack of any training in what used to be confidently called the "canon of evidence"—even more, the disrespect for any such canon—is itself a fact of considerable importance in the training (or non-training) of young historians. This methodological liberation has done more to transform the profession, making it less of a "discipline" and more of an impressionistic "art," than any conscious conversion to postmodernism. It may, indeed, prove to be the lasting influence of postmodernism.

But what of postmodernism itself? Will it last? Is it just another of those intellectual fashions that periodically seize the imagination of a bored and fickle academia? Whatever happened to existentialism? In France, the source of most of these fashions, deconstruction is already passé. Can it survive much longer here? Given the volatility of intellectual and academic life, it is hard not to anticipate a not so distant future when postmodernism will be succeeded by something proudly calling itself "post-postmodernism."

In history, as in literature and philosophy, there almost certainly will be—the signs are already here—a disaffection with postmodernism, if only because the appeal of novelty will wear off.[57] The "herd of independent minds," in Harold Rosenberg's brilliant phrase, will find some other brave new cause to rally around. Out of boredom, careerism (the search for new ways to make a mark in the profession), and sheer bloody-mindedness (the desire to *épater* one's elders), the young will rebel, and the vanguard of today will find itself an aging rear guard—much as the "new history" (social history) of an earlier generation has been displaced by this newer (postmodernist) history. What is not at all clear, however, is the nature and degree of the rebellion—whether it will be a counter-revolution leading to a restoration (or partial restoration) of an older mode of history, or whether it will usher in a still newer mode, the configuration of which we cannot begin to imagine.

One might think that a counter-revolution is already under way in the form of the "new historicism," a linguistic version of Marxism which interprets "cultural productions" as the symbolic forms of material productions. But while some of the members of this school (Frederic Jameson and Terry Eagleton, most notably) criticize postmodernism for being excessively aesthetic and insufficiently revolutionary, they are also attracted to those aspects of it that they recognize as truly subversive. Thus Eagleton praises feminist postmodernism not only for insisting that women have equal power and status with men, but for questioning the legitimacy of *all* power and status. "It is not that the world will be better off with more female participation in it; it is that without the 'feminization' of human history, the world is unlikely to survive."[58] In the common cause of radicalism, structuralists and poststructuralists, new historicists and de-constructionists, have been able to overlook whatever logical incompatibilities there may be between their theories. (This presents no great problem for deconstructionists, who have an infinite tolerance for contradiction and no regard for "linear" logic.) Like the communists and socialists of an earlier generation, they have formed a "popular front," marching separately to a common goal. Thus the new historicism, so far from presenting a real alternative to postmodernism, has become an ally of it, if a somewhat uneasy one. One critic complains of the merger of Marxism and deconstruction, producing the latest oxymoron, "materialist deconstruction."[59]

It is a cliché—and a true one—that no counter-revolution is ever quite that, that the status quo ante is never fully restored. In the case of history, what will stand in the way of a restoration of traditional history is not, as one might think, ideology; one can foresee a desire to return to a more objective and integrated, less divisive and particularistic history. What will be more difficult to restore is the methodology that is at the heart of that history. A generation of historians (by now, several generations as these are reckoned in academia) lacks any training in that methodology. They may even lack the discipline, moral as well as professional, required for it. When Eagleton speaks of the "laid-back" style of postmodernism, he does not mean that it is casual, colloquial, or commonsensical—on the contrary, by normal standards of discourse, it is contrived, abstruse, and recondite—but rather that it is infinitely pluralistic and heterogeneous, renouncing all pretense of rational, "enlightened" discourse.[60] In the case of history, it has meant abandoning not only the conventions regarding the presentation and documentation of evidence, but the very idea of objective evidence, reasoning, coherence, consistency, factuality. The postmodernist argument is that these are the "totalizing," "terroristic" practices of an "authoritarian" discipline.* But they are also the hard practices of a difficult discipline. Gresham's law applies in history as surely as in economics: bad habits drive out good; easy methods drive out hard ones. And there is no doubt that the old history, traditional history, *is* hard.

Hard—but exciting precisely because it is hard. And that excitement may prove a challenge and inspiration for a new generation of historians. It is more exciting to write true history (or as true as we can make it) than fictional history, else historians would choose to be novelists rather than historians; more exciting to try to rise above our interests and prejudices than to indulge them; more exciting to enter the imagination of those remote from us in time and place than to impose our imagination upon them; more exciting to write a coherent narrative while respecting the complexity of historical events than to fragmentize history into disconnected units; more exciting to try to get the facts (without benefit of quotation marks) as right as we can than to deny the very idea of facts; even more exciting to get the footnotes right, if only to show others the visible proof of our labors.

The American political theorist William Dunning said that one of the happiest days of his life was when he discovered, by a comparison of handwriting, that Andrew Johnson's

---

*It is curious to find Foucault and Derrida trading these charges against each other. Derrida accuses Foucault of a "logocentrism" and "structuralist totalitarianism . . . similar to the violences of the classical age."[61] Foucault, in turn, charges Derrida with exercising a "limitless sovereignty" over the text, permitting him to "restate" it "indefinitely."[62] On another occasion Foucault describes Derrida's rhetoric as "*obscurantisme terroriste.*" He writes so obscurely, Foucault complains, that one cannot figure out exactly what he is saying, and then, when one criticizes it, he replies, "You don't understand, you are an idiot."[63]

first message to Congress was actually drafted by George Bancroft. "I don't believe," he wrote to his wife, "you can form any idea of the pleasure it gives me to have discovered this little historical fact."[64] Every serious historian has had this experience—the pleasure of discovering a fact that may appear in the published work in a subordinate clause or footnote, but that, however trivial in itself, validates the entire enterprise, because it is not only new but also true.

Postmodernism entices us with the siren call of liberation and creativity, but it may be an invitation to intellectual and moral suicide. Postmodernists boast that in rejecting metaphysics, they are also delivering themselves from humanism. In his essay "The Ends of Man" (playing upon the two meanings of "ends"), Derrida quotes Heidegger approvingly, "Every humanism is metaphysical," and goes on to explain that metaphysics is "the other name of ontotheology."[65] Similarly, Foucault, in his celebrated account of "the end of man," mocks those who cling to the old humanism.

> To all those who still wish to talk about man, about his reign or his liberation, to all those who still ask themselves questions about what man is in his essence, to all those who wish to take him as their starting-point in their attempts to reach the truth . . . to all these warped and twisted forms of reflection we can answer only with a philosophical laugh—which means, to a certain extent, a silent one.[66]

A corollary of the end of man is the end of history. If the liberation from metaphysics means a liberation from humanism, it also means a liberation from history. Hayden White commends those historians of the nineteenth century who "interpreted the burden of the historian as a moral charge to free men from the burden of history."[67] One may think it bizarre to attribute that intention to Tocqueville, among others, but one cannot doubt that that it is indeed the aim of postmodernism. To free men from the "burden" of history is to free them from the burden of humanity. Liberationist history, like liberationist theology, is not a new and higher form of the discipline; it is the negation of the discipline.

If we have survived the "death of God" and the "death of man," we will surely survive the "death of history"—and of truth, reason, morality, society, reality, and all the other verities we used to take for granted and that have now been "problematized" and "deconstructed." We will even survive the death of postmodernism.

Notes

Complete bibliographical information for each reference appears in the first citation of that source in each chapter.

Introduction

1. Lionel Trilling, "Manners, Morals, and the Novel" (1947), in *The Liberal Imagination: Essays on Literature and Society* (New York, 1950), pp. 221–22.
2. Trilling, "Tacitus Now" (1942), in *The Liberal Imagination: Essays on Literature and Society* (New York, 1950), p. 201.
3. See, for example, Trilling's preface to *The Liberal Imagination*, and his novel, *The Middle of the Journey*.
4. See below, pp. 13–16.
5. The original version appeared under the title "The Abyss Revisited" in *The American Scholar*, Summer 1992.
6. Trilling, "On the Teaching of Modern Literature" (1961), in *Beyond Culture: Essays on Literature and Learning* (New York, 1965), p. 27.
7. This was published in *Commentary*, June 1991.
8. This essay has not been published before.
9. This essay appeared in *The American Scholar*, Autumn 1993. A German version is in *Die liberale Gesellschaft*, ed. Krzysztof Michalski (Munich, 1993).
10. This essay was published in *The National Interest*, Summer 1993.
11. Trilling, "Reality in America" (1940), in *The Liberal Imagination*, p. 11.

12. This essay appeared in *The New York Times Book Review*, June 16, 1991.

13. Earlier versions of this essay appeared as "Tradition and Creativity in the Writing of History" in *First Things*, November 1992, and "Telling It as You Like It" in *The Times Literary Supplement*, October 16, 1992.

Chapter I: *On Looking into the Abyss*

1. Lionel Trilling, "On the Teaching of Modern Literature" (1961), in *Beyond Culture: Essays on Literature and Learning* (New York, 1965), p. 27. The original title of Trilling's essay was "On the Modern Element in Modern Literature," a variation on Arnold's inaugural lecture, "On the Modern Element in Literature."

2. *Ibid.*, p. 26.

3. Friedrich Nietzsche, *Thus Spake Zarathustra*, trans. Thomas Common, in *The Philosophy of Nietzsche* (Modern Library ed., New York, n.d.), p. 29 (prologue, ch. iv); p. 165 (part 3, ch. xlvi); p. 286 (part 4, ch. lxxiii, no. 2); p. 287 (part 4, ch. lxxiii, no. 4).

4. Nietzsche, *Birth of Tragedy*, trans. Francis Golffing (Anchor ed., New York, 1956), pp. 60–61 (ch. 9); p. 86 (ch. 14); p. 124 (ch. 21).

5. Trilling, "James Joyce in His Letters" (1968), in *The Last Decade: Essays and Reviews, 1965–75* (New York, 1978), p. 30.

6. Nietzsche, *Birth of Tragedy*, p. 135 (ch. 22).

7. Jonathan Culler, *The Pursuit of Signs: Semiotics, Literature, Deconstruction* (Ithaca, N.Y., 1981), ch. 1; Culler, *Framing the Sign: Criticism and Its Institutions* (Norman, Okla., 1988), p. 40.

8. Gerald Graff, *Professing Literature: An Institutional History* (Chicago, 1987), pp. 252ff. See also Graff, *Beyond the Culture Wars: How Teaching the Conflict Can Revitalize American Education* (New York, 1992).

9. Barbara Herrnstein Smith, *Contingencies of Value: Alternative Perspectives for Critical Theory* (Cambridge, Mass., 1988), p. 5.

10. Elizabeth Connell Fentress, "Why I Left Graduate School," *New Criterion*, June 1989, p. 78.

11. Stanley Fish, *Is There a Text in This Class?* (Cambridge, Mass., 1980), p. 180.

12. Richard King, "The Discipline of Fact/ The Freedom of Fiction," *Journal of American Studies* (Cambridge, Eng.), 1991, p. 172.

13. Jacques Derrida, *Glas* (Paris, 1974), p. 7.

14. Geoffrey H. Hartman, *Criticism in Wilderness: The Study of Literature Today* (New Haven, 1980), pp. 138–41, 207–8, 210, 264.

15. Hartman et al., *Deconstruction and Criticism* (New York, 1990 [1st ed., 1979]), p. ix.

16. Hartman, "Blindness and Insight," *New Republic*, March 7, 1988, p. 29.

17. This account is based upon Miller's essay "On Edge: The Crossways of Contemporary Criticism," in *Romanticism and Contemporary Criticism*, ed. Morris Eaves and Michael Fischer (Ithaca, N.Y., 1986), pp. 102–11. For a summary of the traditional as well as deconstructionist interpretation of this poem, see David Lehman, *Signs of the Times: Deconstruction and the Fall of Paul de Man* (New York, 1991), pp. 125–29.

18. Trilling, "The Two Environments" (1965), in *Beyond Culture*, p. 231.

19. Hartman, "The State of the Art of Criticism," in *The Future of Literary Theory*, ed. Ralph Cohen (1989), p. 100.

20. Hartman, *Saving the Test: Literature/ Derrida/ Philosophy* (Baltimore, 1981), p. 151. Hartman speaks of "the abysm of words" in his introduction to *Deconstruction and Criticism*, p. ix.

21. Jacques Derrida, *Of Grammatology*, trans. Gayatri Chakravorty Spivak (Baltimore, 1976), p. lxxvii.

22. Lehman, pp. 155–56.

23. Nietzsche, "On Truth and Falsity in an Extra-Moral Sense," in *Early Greek Philosophy and Other Essays*, trans. M. A. Mügge, in *The Complete Works of Friedrich Nietzsche*, ed. Oscar Levy (New York, 1964), II, 180.

24. Martin Heidegger, *Poetry, Language, Thought*, trans. Albert Hofstadter (New York, 1971), pp. 191–92.

25. Karl Marx, *The German Ideology*, in Karl Marx and Friedrich Engels, *Basic Writings on Politics and Philosophy*, ed. Lewis S. Feuer (New York, 1959), p. 248.

26. Richard Rorty, *Essays on Heidegger and Others* (Philosophical Papers, vol. II) (Cambridge, Eng., 1991), p. 86.

27. Derrida, "White Mythology: Metaphor in the Text of Philosophy," *New Literary History*, 1974, p. 11.

28. Rorty, *Essays on Heidegger*, p. 86.

29. Rorty, *Objectivity, Relativism, and Truth* (Philosophical Papers, vol. I) (Cambridge, Eng., 1991), pp. 99–102.

30. *Ibid.*, p. 110.

31. *Ibid.*, p. 194.

32. Rorty, "Taking Philosophy Seriously," *New Republic*, April 11, 1988, pp. 31–34.

33. Rorty, "Truth and Freedom: A Reply to Thomas McCarthy," *Critical Inquiry*, Spring 1990, pp. 638–39.

34. Victor Farias, *Heidegger and Nazism*, ed. Joseph Margolis and Tom Rockmore; trans. Paul Burrell and Gabriel R. Ricci (Philadelphia, 1989 [1st ed., 1987]), pp. 283, 287.

35. For a discussion of structuralism and history, see Chapter II, "Of Heroes, Villains, and Valets"; and for deconstruction, see Chapter VII, "Postmodernist History."

36. Charles S. Maier, *The Unmasterable Past: History, Holocaust, and German National Identity* (Cambridge, Mass., 1988), pp. 36–37.

37. Dan Diner, "Between Aporia and Apology: On the Limits of Historicizing National Socialism," in *Reworking the Past: Hitler, the Holocaust, and the Historians' Debate*, ed. Peter Baldwin (Boston, 1990), p. 139.

38. Mary Nolan, "The *Historikerstreit* and Social History," in *Reworking the Past*, p. 243.

39. Diner, p. 140. See also David F. Crew, "*Alltagsgeschichte*: A New Social History 'from Below'?," *Central European History*, September/December 1989.

40. See Chapter VII, "Postmodernist History," pp. 142–46.

41. Derrida, "Like the Sound of the Sea Deep Within a Shell:

Paul de Man's War," in *Responses on Paul de Man's Wartime Journalism*, ed. Werner Hamacher *et al.* (Lincoln, Nebr., 1989), pp. 129, 143, 149, 154, 157, 164 (n. 44). (This article appeared earlier in *Critical Inquiry*, Spring 1988.)

42. Jean-François Lyotard, *Heidegger and "the jews,"* trans. Andreas Michel and Mark S. Roberts (Minneapolis, 1990), p. xxviii (interview by Jacques Derrida, quoted in the Foreword by David Carroll). See also Thomas Sheehan, "A Normal Nazi," *New York Review of Books*, January 14, 1993, p. 31.

43. Ortwin de Graef, "Aspects of the Context of Paul de Man's Earliest Publications," *Responses*, p. 113. It was de Graef, a young scholar and admirer of de Man, who first discovered these articles.

44. S. Heidi Krueger, "Opting to Know: On the Wartime Journalism of Paul de Man," *ibid.*, p. 307.

45. David H. Hirsch, *The Deconstruction of Literature: Criticism After Auschwitz* (Hanover, N.H., 1991), pp. 108–9, quoting Leon S. Roudiez, "Searching for Achilles' Heel: Paul de Man's Disturbing Youth," *World Literature Today*, 1989, p. 439.

46. Hartman, *Minor Prophecies: The Literary Essay in the Culture Wars* (Cambridge, Mass., 1991), pp. 124–25.

47. Hartman, "Blindness and Insight," *New Republic*, p. 30. These and other points are developed at much greater length in Hartman's *Minor Prophecies*, pp. 123–48.

48. Shoshana Felman, "Paul de Man's Silence," *Critical Inquiry*, Summer 1989, p. 733. (The italics are the author's.)

49. J. Hillis Miller, "An Open Letter to Professor Jon Wiener," *Responses*, p. 334; *Times Literary Supplement*, June 17–23, 1988, p. 685.

50. Derrida, *Responses*, p. 160 (n. 44).

51. Miller, *The Ethics of Reading* (New York, 1987), p. 58.

52. For a discussion of other aspects of this book, see Chapter VII, "Postmodernist History."

53. David Abraham, *The Collapse of the Weimar Republic: Political Economy and Crisis* (Princeton, 1981).

54. Natalie Zemon Davis, "About Dedications," *Radical History Review*, March 1985, pp. 94–96.

55. *Ibid.*, pp. 95–96.

56. Nietzsche, *Beyond Good and Evil*, trans. Helen Zimmern (Modern Library ed., n.d.), p. 87 (ch. iv, no. 146).

Chapter II: *Of Heroes, Villains, and Valets*

1. It has also been attributed to Madame de Sévigné's contemporaries Madame Cornuel and the Duc de Condé.
2. Georg Wilhelm Friedrich Hegel, *Phenomenology of Spirit*, trans. A. V. Miller (Oxford, 1977), p. 404; *Philosophy of History*, trans. J. Sibree (New York, 1944), p. 32.
3. Hegel, *Philosophy of History*, p. 32.
4. *Ibid.*
5. Hegel, *Phenomenology of Spirit*, p. 404.
6. Byron, "Beppo," stanza 32.
7. Hegel, *Philosophy of History*, p. 31.
8. Hegel, *Philosophy of Right*, trans. T. M. Knox (Oxford, 1942), p. 245 (Additions no. 58).
9. Aristotle, *Nicomachean Ethics*, trans. Hippocrates G. Apostle (Grinnell, Iowa, 1975), p. 175 (Book 4, 1123b).
10. *Letters and Journals of Lord Byron*, ed. Thomas Moore (London, 1875), I, 435. I am indebted to Richard D. Altick, *Lives and Letters: A History of Literary Biography in England and America* (New York, 1965), for suggesting this and other sources.
11. Howard Mumford Jones, *The Harp That Once* (New York, 1970 [1st ed., 1937]), p. 352 (n. 6).
12. Hallam Tennyson, *Alfred Lord Tennyson: A Memoir* (London, 1897), II, 165.
13. Thomas Carlyle, *Heroes, Hero-Worship and the Heroic in History* (New York, n.d. [1st ed., 1841]), p. 14.
14. *Ibid.*, p. 217.
15. *Ibid.*, pp. 14–15.
16. James Anthony Froude, *Thomas Carlyle: A History of the First Forty Years of His Life, 1795–1835* (London, 1882), I, ix–xii (quoting Carlyle's review of John Gibson Lockhart's *Life of Sir Walter Scott*).
17. John Morley, *Voltaire* (London, 1872), pp. 97–98.

18. Virginia Woolf, "Mr. Bennett and Mrs. Brown" (1924), in *Collected Essays* (New York, 1967), I, 320.
19. Woolf, "The Art of Biography," in *Collected Essays*, IV, 227.
20. Woolf, "The New Biography" (1927), in *Collected Essays*, IV, 231.
21. Michael Holroyd, *Lytton Strachey: A Critical Biography* (New York, 1967–68), II, 261.
22. Lytton Strachey, *Eminent Victorians: Cardinal Manning, Florence Nightingale, Dr. Arnold, General Gordon* (New York, n.d.), p. 210.
23. *Ibid.*, p. 264.
24. *Ibid.*, p. 39.
25. *Ibid.*, p. 193.
26. See Gertrude Himmelfarb, *The New History and the Old* (Cambridge, Mass., 1987), pp. 1–3, for the earlier appearance of the "new history." It was another "new historian," Carl Becker, who used that term in reviewing Wells's book. ("Mr. Wells and the New History" [1921], reprinted in *Everyman His Own Historian: Essays on History and Politics* [Chicago, 1966].)
27. H. G. Wells, *Outline of History* (New York, 1971 [1st ed., 1920]), pp. 779–80.
28. John P. Sisk, "Biography Without End," *Antioch Review*, 1990, p. 449. Sisk attributes the word to Joyce Carol Oates in her review of David Roberts's biography of Jean Stafford. ("Pathography" was occasionally used in the nineteenth century in the literal medical sense, meaning the description of a disease.)
29. E. P. Thompson, *The Making of the English Working Class* (New York, 1964), p. 12.
30. On Columbus, see Robert Royal, *1492 and All That: Political Manipulations of History* (Lanham, Md., 1992); and on the Armada, see David Starkey in *The Times Literary Supplement*, Dec. 2–8, 1988, pp. 1346–47.
31. G. R. Elton, *Political History: Principles and Practice* (New York, 1970), pp. 70–71. The most recent exercise in the denigration of Churchill is John Charmley, *Churchill: The End of Glory: A Political Biography* (London, 1993). The lead editorial in *The*

Times, prior to the serialization of this book in *The Sunday Times*, explains that "revisionism is valuable, even when the conclusions are wrong" (January 6, 1993).

32. Quoted in Himmelfarb, *The New History and the Old*, p. 31.

33. This production, needless to say, did not escape the vigil of the "revisionists." See, for example, Jeanie Attie, "Illusions of History: A Review of *The Civil War*," *Radical History Review*, Winter 1992.

34. Alexis de Tocqueville, *Democracy in America*, ed. J. P. Mayer and Max Lerner; trans. George Lawrence (New York, 1966), pp. 462–63 (vol. II, part 1, ch. 20).

35. *Ibid.*, p. 465.

36. For an analysis of this school, see Lucy S. Dawidowicz, *The War Against the Jews: 1933–1945* (New York, 1975), and *The Holocaust and the Historians* (Cambridge, Mass., 1981); Michael R. Marrus, *The Holocaust in History* (Hanover, N.H., 1987); Charles S. Maier, *The Unmasterable Past: History, Holocaust, and German National Identity* (Cambridge, Mass., 1988); Peter Baldwin, ed., *Reworking the Past: Hitler, the Holocaust, and the Historians' Debate* (Boston, 1990).

37. Dawidowicz, *The War Against the Jews* (1986 edition), p. xxvii.

38. For a discussion of other modes of interpreting Nazism and the Holocaust, which also have the effect of trivializing and "demoralizing" it, see Chapter I, "On Looking into the Abyss," and Chapter VII, "Postmodernist History."

39. Sheila Fitzpatrick, "New Perspectives on Stalinism," *Russian Review*, 1986, pp. 367–69. (Replies to Fitzpatrick appear in this and subsequent issues of this journal.) See also Lynn Viola, *The Best Sons of the Fatherland: Workers in the Vanguard of Soviet Collectivization* (New York, 1987); Terence Emmons, "The Abusable Past," *The New Republic*, March 9, 1992, p. 33.

40. Kevin Tyner Thomas, "On the Politics of Interpretation: Robert Conquest and the Historiography of Stalinism," *Radical History Review*, Winter 1992, pp. 124–25.

41. Fitzpatrick, p. 369.

42. Alfred G. Meyer, "Coming to Terms with the Past . . . And

with One's Older Colleagues," *Russian Review*, 1986, p. 406. This is Meyer's paraphrase (cited in criticism) of a statement by Theo von Laue in "Stalin in Focus," *Slavic Review*, 1983.

43. Robert Conquest, "The Party in the Dock," *The Times Literary Supplement*, November 6, 1992, p. 7. See also Richard Pipes, "Seventy-five Years On," in the same issue, pp. 3–4.

44. Peter Kenez, "Stalinism as Humdrum Politics," *Russian Review*, 1986, pp. 399–400.

45. Terence Emmons, review of Richard Pipes, *The Russian Revolution*, in *The New Republic*, November 5, 1990, p. 38.

46. Fernand Braudel, *On History*, trans. Sarah Matthews (Chicago, 1980), pp. 10–11.

47. Braudel, "Personal Testimony," *Journal of Modern History*, 1972, p. 454.

48. Tacitus, *The Annals*, trans. Alfred John Church and William Jackson Brodribb (Vol. XV of Great Books ed., Chicago, 1952), p. 60 (Book 3, par. 65).

49. Trilling, "Tacitus Now" (1942), in *The Liberal Imagination: Essays on Literature and Society* (New York, 1950), p. 201.

50. Robert Langbaum, "The Importance of *The Liberal Imagination*," *Salmagundi*, 1978, p. 65.

Chapter III: *From Marx to Hegel*

1. *Washington Post*, February 23, 1990.

2. After writing this, I discovered that "From Marx to Hegel" is the title of a book of essays by George Lichtheim (London, 1971). In the title essay, Lichtheim focuses on three contemporary thinkers who, in different ways, "Hegelianized" Marx: Georg Lukács, Theodor Adorno, and Herbert Marcuse.

3. Perhaps the earliest account in English of the "young Marx" and his relations to the Young Hegelians is Sidney Hook, *From Hegel to Marx: Studies in the Intellectual Development of Karl Marx* (New York, 1936). For a summary of the rediscovery of the young Marx, see Daniel Bell, *The End of Ideology* (Glencoe, Ill.,

1960); Robert Tucker, *Philosophy and Myth in Karl Marx* (Cambridge, Eng., 1961). There is by now a voluminous literature both on the Young Hegelians of Marx's time and the neo-Marxists of our own.

4. Bell, p. 343.

5. Karl Marx, *The Communist Manifesto*, ed. Samuel H. Beer (New York, 1955), p. 37.

6. Those associated with the Frankfurt group (Theodor Adorno, Max Horkheimer) were always interested in Hegel, but it was not until after the war, when most of them took up residence in the West, that they became influential outside their own circle. It was also just after the war that Alexandre Kojève introduced to France a Marxized Hegel.

7. Georg Wilhelm Friedrich Hegel, *The Philosophy of History*, trans. J. Sibree (New York, 1944), p. 9. (I have lowercased most of the nouns, except those—such as "Reason" in this quotation—that in the context have a special emphasis and significance.)

8. *Ibid.*, p. 36.

9. *Ibid.*, p. 20.

10. *Ibid.*, p. 27.

11. *Ibid.*, pp. 29–30.

12. Hegel, *Reason in History: A General Introduction to the Philosophy of History*, trans. and ed. Robert S. Hartman (Library of Liberal Arts, 1953), p. xvii.

13. Hegel, *The Philosophy of History*, p. 18. (Italics here and in all other quotations are in the original.)

14. Ludwig Feuerbach, *The Essence of Christianity*, trans. George Eliot (New York, 1957 [1st ed., 1841), p. 271.

15. Max Stirner, *The Ego and His Own*, ed. John Carroll (New York, 1971 [1st ed., 1845]), p. 251.

16. *Ibid.*, p. 261.

17. *The Communist Manifesto*, p. 9.

18. *Ibid.*, p. 15.

19. Karl Marx and Friedrich Engels, *The German Ideology*, in *Basic Writings on Politics and Philosophy*, ed. Lewis S. Feuer (New York, 1959), p. 257.

20. *The Communist Manifesto*, pp. 25, 16.

21. *Ibid.*, pp. 21, 27.
22. *Ibid.*, pp. 27–29.
23. Engels, *The Condition of the Working Class in England*, in Marx and Engels, *Collected Works* (New York, 1975), IV, 419–20, 425–27, 437–41.
24. *The German Ideology*, in *Basic Writings*, p. 257.
25. *Ibid.*, p. 248.
26. *The Communist Manifesto*, p. 27.
27. *Ibid.*, p. 25.
28. *Ibid.*, pp. 30–31.
29. *Ibid.*, p. 32. (This is the final sentence before the appendix on other schools of socialism and communism.)
30. *The German Ideology*, in *Basic Writings*, p. 254.
31. *Ibid.*, p. 247.
32. *The Communist Manifesto*, p. 27.
33. *Ibid.*, p. 42.
34. *Ibid.*, p. 23.
35. Hannah Arendt, *The Human Condition* (Chicago, 1958), pp. 101ff.
36. *The Communist Manifesto*, p. 16.
37. *Toward the Critique of Hegel's Philosophy of Right*, in *Basic Writings*, pp. 264–65. (I have eliminated most of the italics in this passage because they are distracting.)

Chapter IV: *Liberty: "One Very Simple Principle"?*

1. If popular government was a settled issue, the best form of such a government was not. Mill addressed this subject in a pamphlet, *Thoughts on Parliamentary Government*, published a few months after *On Liberty*, and at greater length two years later in *Considerations on Representative Government*.
2. John Stuart Mill, *On Liberty* (Everyman ed., London, 1910), p. 68.
3. *On Liberty*, p. 65. Ronald Dworkin concedes that while Mill's principle may seem absolute, this is of little significance because the principle itself is of "very limited range."

It speaks only to those relatively rare occasions when a government is asked to prohibit some act on the sole ground that the act is dangerous to the actor, like driving a motorcycle without a helmet. Or on the ground that it is offensive to community standards of morality, like practicing homosexuality or publishing or reading pornography. Such decisions form a very small part of the business of any responsible government. . . . The more limited the range of a principle, the more plausibly it may be said to be absolute. (*Taking Rights Seriously* [Cambridge, Mass., 1977], p. 261.)

It is doubtful that Mill would have appreciated a defense of his principle on the ground that it was of such a "limited range" and applied to such "rare occasions" as not wearing a helmet while driving a motorcycle—especially because he explicitly, in the opening sentence of his book, gave it a very considerable range— not only in respect to the power of government but to that of society.

4. *On Liberty*, pp. 72–73.

5. *Ibid.*, p. 73. Later in the essay, Mill defines "maturity" as referring to persons "of full age, and the ordinary amount of understanding" (p. 132).

6. Henry Magid, "John Stuart Mill," in *History of Political Philosophy*, ed. Leo Strauss and Joseph Cropsey (3rd ed., Chicago, 1987), p. 799.

7. *On Liberty*, p. 75.

8. *Ibid.*, pp. 98, 111, 95.

9. E.g., Dworkin, pp. 262–63.

10. John Milton, *Areopagitica*, in *The Prose of John Milton*, ed. J. Max Patrick (New York, 1968), p. 272; John Locke, *An Essay Concerning the True Original, Extent, and End of Civil Government* (The Second Treatise), in *Two Treatises of Government*, ed. Peter Laslett (Cambridge, Eng., 1967), p. 288 (ch. II, no. 6); Charles de Secondat, Baron de Montesquieu, *The Spirit of the Laws*, trans. Thomas Nugent, ed. Franz Neumann (New York, 1949), p. 109

(Book VIII, no. 2). (I have modernized the spelling and capitalization where necessary.)

11. *On Liberty*, pp. 115–25. This belies the theory of some commentators that Mill was an "elitist," intending his principle of liberty only for those superior individuals who could make the best use of it. Joseph Hamburger, for example, maintains that *On Liberty* was meant to show how those persons with "desirable individuality" would prevail over those with "miserable individuality," thus contributing to the "reconstruction of the human intellect." (*How Liberal Was John Stuart Mill?* [Austin, Tex., 1991], p. 15). But it is only by citing the "other Mill," as I have called him—his quotations are from *Utilitarianism* and Mill's private diary—that this interpretation can be supported.

12. Milton, p. 330.

13. *On Liberty*, p. 68. The influence of Tocqueville on Mill is indisputable. Mill had written lengthy essays on the two volumes of Tocqueville's *Democracy in America*, in 1835 and 1840. The second of these essays was reprinted in his *Dissertations and Discussions* in 1859, the very year of *On Liberty*.

14. Benedict de Spinoza, *Tractatus Theologicus Politicus*, in *The Political Works of Spinoza*, trans. A. G. Wernham (Oxford, 1958), p. 231.

15. Locke, *A Letter Concerning Toleration*, ed. Patrick Romanell (New York, 1861), p. 52.

16. Montesquieu, *The Spirit of the Laws*, p. 150 (Book XI, no. 3).

17. Immanuel Kant, "What Is Enlightenment?" in *The Philosophy of Kant: Immanuel Kant's Moral and Political Writings*, ed. Carl J. Friedrich (Modern Library ed., New York, 1949).

18. *Writings of Thomas Jefferson*, ed. H. A. Washington (New York, 1861), II, 99–100; Thomas Paine, *Common Sense and the Crisis* (New York, 1960), p. 13, and *The Rights of Man* (Penguin ed., London, 1969), pp. 185ff.

19. "Conversation Between Mr. Cowley and Mr. Milton," *The Works of Lord Macaulay* (London, 1875), VII, 658.

20. Alexis de Tocqueville, *Democracy in America*, trans. Henry Reeve, ed. Phillips Bradley (New York, 1948), I, 12.

21. Edward Gibbon, *Autobiography*, ed. Lord Sheffield (World's Classics ed., London, 1950), p. 160.

22. Mill, *Autobiography*, ed. John Jacob Coss (New York, 1924), p. 170.

23. *The Later Letters of John Stuart Mill: 1849–1873*, ed. Francis E. Mineka and Dwight N. Lindley, in *Collected Works*, vol. XIV (Toronto, 1972), p. 294.

24. *Letters of Lord Acton to Mary Gladstone*, ed. Herbert Paul (New York, 1905), p. 99.

25. *On Liberty*, p. 114.

26. *Ibid.*, p. 135.

27. *Ibid.*, p. 132.

28. *Ibid.*, p. 137–38, 132.

29. *Ibid.*, pp. 118–19.

30. Mill, *Essays on Ethics, Religion and Society*, ed. J. M. Robson, in *Collected Works*, vol. X (Toronto, 1969), pp. 392–401.

31. Friedrich Nietzsche, *The Will to Power*, trans. and ed. Walter Kaufmann (New York, 1967), p. 21 (no. 30), p. 186 (no. 340); *Twilight of the Idols*, in *The Portable Nietzsche*, ed. Walter Kaufmann (New York, 1954), pp. 515–16 (no. 5).

32. *On Liberty*, pp. 85–92.

33. *Ibid.*, pp. 91–92.

34. *Ibid.*, p. 92.

35. *Ibid.*, p. 131. (This is the title of chapter IV.)

36. *Ibid.*, p. 153.

37. *Ibid.*

38. *Ibid.*

39. *Ibid.*, p. 154.

40. Machiavelli, *Political Discourses upon the First Decade of Livy*, in *The Works of Nicholas Machiavel* (London, 1762), II, 56 (chap. 18).

41. Thomas Hobbes, *Leviathan* (Everyman ed., London, 1914), p. 49.

42. *On Liberty*, p. 150.

43. *Ibid.*, pp. 164–65.

44. For a detailed discussion of Mill's views on socialism, see Gertrude Himmelfarb, *On Liberty and Liberalism: The Case of John*

Stuart Mill (New York, 1974), pp. 126–39, and *Poverty and Compassion: The Moral Imagination of the Late Victorians* (New York, 1991), pp. 263–69.

45. Patrick Devlin, *The Enforcement of Morals* (Oxford, 1965), pp. 133–35.

46. Milton, p. 271.

47. Montesquieu, p. 40 (Book V, no. 2), p. 111 (Book VIII, no. 3).

48. *The Federalist*, ed. Jacob E. Cooke (Middletown, Conn., 1972), *Federalist* 57, p. 384.

49. Jonathan Eliott, ed., *The Debates in the Several State Conventions, on the Adoption of the Federal Constitution* (Philadelphia, 1907), III, 536–37.

50. Tocqueville, II, 98 (vol. II, Book II, ch. 2).

51. *Ibid.*, I, 305–6 (ch. 17).

52. *Ibid.*, II, 3–6 (Book I, ch. 1).

53. *Ibid.*, I, 44 (ch. 2).

54. *Ibid.*, I, 307 (ch. 17).

55. George Washington, Farewell Address, in *The Writings of George Washington*, ed. John C. Fitzpatrick (Washington, 1940), XXXV, 229.

56. For a more extended discussion of the "other Mill," see Himmelfarb, *On Liberty and Liberalism*; and for a critique of this view, C. L. Ten, *Mill on Liberty* (Oxford, 1980), pp. 151–73.

57. Mill, *Autobiography*, p. 111; *The Earlier Letters of John Stuart Mill, 1812–1848*, ed. Francis E. Mineka, in *Collected Works*, vol. XII (Toronto, 1963), p. 36.

58. Mill, "The Spirit of the Age," in *Essays on Politics and Culture*, ed. Gertrude Himmelfarb (New York, 1962), p. 15.

59. Mill, "Coleridge," in *Essays on Politics and Culture*, p. 138.

60. Mill, "Utilitarianism," in *Essays on Ethics, Religion and Society*, pp. 218, 231.

61. *Ibid.*, pp. 231, 216.

62. Mill, *Earlier Letters*, I, 36. See also *Representative Government* (Everyman ed., London, 1910), p. 193.

63. Mill, "Coleridge," in *Essays on Politics and Culture*, pp. 136–42.

64. See Chapter III, "From Marx to Hegel," p. 50.

65.   Václav Havel, "Paradise Lost," *New York Review of Books*, April 9, 1992, p. 6.

Chapter V: *The Dark and Bloody Crossroads*
Where Nationalism and Religion Meet

1.   E. H. Carr, *Nationalism and After* (London, 1945), pp. 36–37.
2.   Theodore Zeldin, "Social History and Total History," *Journal of Social History*, 1976, 242–43.
3.   Theodore Zeldin, review of Robert Blake, ed., *The English World*, *Times Literary Supplement*, December 31, 1982, p. 1436.
4.   Michael Oakeshott, *On History and Other Essays* (Oxford, 1983), p. 100.
5.   The title of Zeldin's first work, *France 1848–1945*, manages to include two of the "tyrannical" categories that he denounces: nationality and chronology.
6.   Benedict Anderson, *Imagined Communities: Reflections on the Origin and Spread of Nationalism* (London, 1983), pp. 13–15.
7.   *Ibid.*, pp. 78, 123.
8.   Eric Hobsbawm and Terence Ranger, eds., *The Invention of Tradition* (Cambridge, Eng., 1983), pp. 2–3, 13, 263. See also Raphael Samuel, ed., *Patriotism: The Making and Unmaking of British National Identity* (London, 1989), I, lx and *passim*; Ernest Gellner, *Thought and Change* (London, 1964), p. 168. In a later book, Gellner denies the artificial or fictitious nature of these "inventions" (*Nations and Nationalism* [Ithaca, 1983], p. 56). Anderson and Hobsbawm coined the terms that popularized this idea of nationalism, but not the idea itself. Two years before their books appeared, a survey of recent literature on nationalism described the "artificial or manufactured character" of nineteenth-century nationalities as the "accepted approaches" to the subject (Geoffrey Eley, "Nationalism and Social History," *Social History*, January 1981, p. 90).
9.   Hobsbawm, *Nations and Nationalism Since 1780: Programme, Myth, Reality* (Cambridge, Eng., 1990), pp. 163, 170. Another prominent English radical recently announced, at the risk of

"virtual excommunication" from his circle (The *New Left Review*), that nationalism in this historical period "may on the whole be preferable to what went before." (Tom Nairn, "Demonising Nationalism," *London Review of Books*, February 25, 1993, p. 5.)

10. Lionel Trilling spoke of "the dark and bloody crossroads where literature and politics meet" ("Reality in America" [1940], in *The Liberal Imagination* [New York, 1950], p. 11).

11. E.g., Elie Kedourie, *Nationalism* (London, 1960); Kenneth Minogue, *Nationalism* (New York, 1967); J. L. Talmon, *The Myth of the Nation and the Vision of Revolution: The Origins of Ideological Polarisation in the Twentieth Century* (London, 1981); Gellner, *Nations and Nationalism* (Ithaca, N.Y., 1983). Anthony D. Smith criticizes the "functionalist" explanation of nationalism as "religion politicized" on the grounds that this is a simplistic view of religion itself. But he himself gives religion only an "indirect, ambiguous and reactive role" in nationalism (*Theories of Nationalism* [London, 1983 (1st ed., 1971)], pp. 54, 57). Eugene Kamenka, on the other hand, predicted, as early as 1973, the emergence of "primary tensions" in Yugoslavia because of religious differences that took the form of national differences (Kamenka, ed., *Nationalism: The Nature and Evolution of an Idea* [London, 1976 (1st ed., 1973)], p. 13). See also Salo Wittmayer Baron, who quotes Leopold von Ranke's observation, in 1872, that "in most periods of world history nations were held together by religious ties alone" (Baron, *Modern Nationalism and Religion* [Freeport, N.Y., 1971 (1st ed., 1947)], p. 20.).

12. Louis L. Snyder, *Encyclopedia of Nationalism* (New York, 1990). In the pioneer work on the subject, Carlton J. H. Hayes laid down the classic typology of nationalism: humanitarian, Jacobin, traditional, liberal, integral, and economic (*Essays on Nationalism* [New York, 1926]). The exclusion of religious nationalism by Hayes is all the more interesting because he himself was a prominent Catholic layman. He believed, however, that the Catholic church, as the leading spiritual force in the world, was a powerful force against nationalism.

13. Liah Greenfeld, *Nationalism: Five Roads to Modernity* (Cambridge, Mass., 1992), p. 23.

14.   Linda Colley, *Britons: Forging the Nation 1707–1837* (New Haven, 1992), pp. 54, 368–69, 374, and *passim*.

15.   Conor Cruise O'Brien, *God Land: Reflections on Religion and Nationalism* (Cambridge, Mass., 1988), pp. 39, 81, and *passim*.

16.   A notable exception is Greenfeld, who reverses the conventional formula, arguing that nationalism is not the product but the precondition of modernization (pp. 18–21 and *passim*). Colley has nationalism predating modernization in its origins but, like most historians, assumes a radical diminution of nationalism as modernization progresses (pp. 369, 374).

17.   Anthony Giddens, *A Contemporary Critique of Historical Materialism*, vol. II, *The Nation-State and Violence* (Oxford, 1986), pp. 73, 218.

18.   Gellner, *Nations and Nationalism*, pp. 34, 40, 142.

19.   Francis Fukuyama, "The End of History?," *The National Interest*, Summer 1989, p. 14.

20.   Fukuyama, *The End of History and the Last Man* (New York, 1992), p. 201.

21.   *Ibid.*, p. 271. Almost half a century ago, Hans Kohn drew a similar parallel between religion and nationalism. The religious wars and the Enlightenment, he wrote, led to the "depoliticization of religion," the severing of the connection between religion and the state, and the retreat of religion into the individual conscience. A similar "depoliticization of nationality" is conceivable now. "It [nationality] may lose its connection with political organization, it may remain an intimate and moving sentiment. If and when that day arrives, however, the age of nationalism, in the sense in which it is considered here, will be past" (*The Idea of Nationalism: A Study in Its Origins and Background* [New York, 1944], pp. 23–24).

22.   Lionel Trilling, "Tacitus Now" (1942), in *The Liberal Imagination: Essays on Literature and Society* (New York, 1950), p. 201.

23.   John Stuart Mill, *Considerations on Representative Government* (Everyman ed., London, n.d. [1st ed., 1861]), pp. 360–64. On the Breton or Basque, Mill was devastatingly candid. How much better it was for him to be absorbed by a higher nationality than to "sulk on his own rocks, the half-savage relic of past times,

revolving in his own little mental orbit, without participation or interest in the general movement of the world."

24. George Orwell, *The Lion and the Unicorn: Socialism and the English Genius* (1941), in *The Collected Essays, Journalism and Letters of George Orwell*, ed. Sonia Orwell and Ian Angus (New York, 1968), II, 75.

Chapter VI: *Where Have All the Footnotes Gone?*

1. A sampling of recent scholarly books sans notes includes: Daniel Boorstin, *The Discoverers* (New York, 1983) and *The Creators* (New York, 1992); Simon Schama, *Citizens: A Chronicle of the French Revolution* (New York, 1989); F.M.L. Thompson, *The Rise of Respectable Society: A Social History of Victorian Britain 1830–1900* (Cambridge, Mass., 1988); Jose Harris, *Private Lives, Public Spirits: A Social History of Britain 1870–1914* (Oxford, 1993); G. E. Mingay, *The Transformation of Britain 1830–1939* (London, 1986); William Appleman Williams, *The Contours of American History* (Cleveland, 1961); Gordon A. Craig, *The Triumph of Liberalism: Zurich in the Golden Age, 1839–1869* (New York, 1988); Arno J. Mayer, *Why Did the Heavens Not Darken? The "Final Solution" in History* (New York, 1988); Stanley Weintraub, *Long Day's Journey into War: December 7, 1941* (New York, 1991); Mary Frances Berry and John W. Blassingame, *Long Memory: The Black Experience in America* (New York, 1982); Peter Ackroyd, *Dickens* (New York, 1990); Michael Holroyd, *Bernard Shaw* (New York, 1988); Robert B. Asprey, *Frederick the Great: The Magnificent Enigma* (New York, 1986). Some of these volumes (by Schama and Ackroyd, for example) have bibliographical essays but not specific notes or page references. Others (by Asprey, for example), have occasional notes citing the source book but not the page or even chapter.

2. Jean-Jacques Rousseau, *The First and Second Discourses*, ed. Roger D. Masters, trans. Roger D. and Judith R. Masters (New York, 1964), p. 98.

3. *Ibid.*, p. 234, n. 18.

4. Kate L. Turabian, *A Manual for Writers of Term Papers, Theses, and Dissertations* (Chicago, 1987). (The first edition, published in 1937, was entitled *A Manual for Writers of Dissertations*.) The manual has been considerably revised over the course of the years, generally in the direction of greater latitude.

5. Asprey, p. 639.

6. Thompson, p. 10.

7. The earlier volumes appeared in 1988, 1989, and 1991. A fourth volume, including the notes, was published in 1993.

8. Boorstin, *The Discoverers*, p. 685.

9. Weintraub, p. 668.

10. Asprey, pp. 639–40.

11. Lucy S. Dawidowicz, *What Is the Use of Jewish History?*, ed. Neal Kozodoy (New York, 1992), p. 123.

12. Williams, p. 491.

13. Wilcomb E. Washburn, quoting the introduction to Allen P. Slickpoo, Sr., and Deward E. Walker, Jr., *Noon Nee-Me-Poo* (1973), in *Idaho Yesterdays: The Quarterly Journal of the Idaho Historical Society*, 1974, p. 30.

14. Alan Watkins, "Diary," *The Spectator*, May 2, 1992, p. 7.

Chapter VII: *Postmodernist History*

1. Ihab Hassan, *The Postmodern Turn: Essays in Postmodern Theory and Culture*, quoted, not ironically, by Gabrielle M. Spiegel, "History and Post-Modernism," *Past and Present*, May 1992, p. 194 (n. 3).

2. T. S. Eliot, "Tradition and the Individual Talent" (1917), in *Selected Essays 1917–1932* (New York, 1932), p. 7.

3. This is the title of Becker's book published that year. Twenty years earlier, Becker had made much the same point in an article in *The Atlantic Monthly*.

4. J. H. Hexter, *On Historians* (Cambridge, Mass., 1979), pp. 16–17.

5. *Ibid.*, pp. 18–19.

6. John Higham, *History* (Englewood, N.J., 1965), p. 90.

7. Theodore Zeldin, "Social History and Total History," *Journal of Social History*, 1976, pp. 242–44.

8. Linda Nochlin, *The Politics of Vision: Essays on Nineteenth-Century Art and Society* (New York, 1989), p. 182.

9. Zeldin, *London Review of Books*, September 1, 1988.

10. Dominick LaCapra, "Rethinking Intellectual History and Reading Texts," in LaCapra and Steven L. Kaplan, eds., *Modern European Intellectual History: Reappraisals and New Perspectives* (Ithaca, N.Y., 1982), p. 78.

11. Hayden White, *Tropics of Discourse: Essays in Cultural Criticism* (Baltimore, 1978), pp. 81ff.

12. White, *Metahistory: The Historical Imagination in Nineteenth-Century Europe* (Baltimore, 1973), pp. 9–10.

13. White, "The Burden of History," *History and Theory*, 1966, p. 129; reprinted in *Tropics of Discourse*, p. 45.

14. Michael Kazin, "The Grass-Roots Right: New Histories of U.S. Conservatism in the Twentieth Century," *American Historical Review*, 1992, p. 155. (The quote about "humane values" is from Gordon Wright's presidential address, *ibid.*, 1976, p. 81.)

15. See Chapter I, "On Looking into the Abyss," for a discussion of another aspect of the Abraham affair.

16. Arno J. Mayer, "A Letter to Henry Turner," *Radical History Review*, 1985, pp. 85–86.

17. Quoted by Jon Wiener, "Footnotes to History," *The Nation*, February 16, 1985.

18. *Ibid.*, p. 182.

19. Thomas Bender, " 'Facts' and History," *Radical History Review*, 1985, pp. 81–83.

20. Henry Ashby Turner, Jr., *German Big Business and the Rise of Hitler* (Oxford, 1985), p. 357.

21. Jane Caplan, "Postmodernism, Poststructuralism, and Deconstruction: Notes for Historians," *Central European History*, September/December 1989, pp. 274, 278.

22. White, "Historical Emplotment and the Problem of Truth," in *Probing the Limits of Representation: Nazism and the "Final Solution*," ed. Saul Friedlander (Cambridge, Mass., 1992), pp. 37ff.

23. *Ibid.*, p. 41.

24. *Ibid.*, pp. 51–52.

25. Martin Jay, "Of Plots, Witnesses, and Judgments," in *Probing the Limits*, p. 97.

26. Carlo Ginzburg, "Just One Witness," in *Probing the Limits*, p. 86. On postmodernism and the Holocaust, see also James E. Young, *Writing and Rewriting the Holocaust: Narrative and the Consequences of Interpretation* (Bloomington, Ind., 1988); David H. Hirsch, *The Deconstruction of Literature: Criticism After Auschwitz* (Hanover, N.H., 1991).

27. Linda Hutcheon, "The Postmodern Problematizing of History," *English Studies in Canada*, December 1988, pp. 371 and *passim* (reprinted in *A Poetics of Postmodernism: History, Theory, Fiction* [New York, 1988]).

28. Ira Bruce Nadel, *Biography: Fiction, Fact and Form* (New York, 1984), pp. 77–78. See also David Lodge, review of a biography of D. H. Lawrence, *New York Review of Books*, February 13, 1992, and Lodge's letter, *New York Review of Books*, April 9, 1992, p. 56, for his own rather tortuous endorsement of this view.

29. Arnaldo Momigliano, "Biblical Studies and Classical Studies: Simple Reflections upon Historical Method" (1981), in *On Pagans, Jews, and Christians* (Middletown, Conn., 1987), p. 5.

30. Quoted by David Bell, "Fallen Idols," *London Review of Books*, July 23, 1992, p. 13.

31. J. H. Plumb, *The Death of the Past* (Boston, 1970), p. 135.

32. Thomas Babington Macaulay, "History" (1828), *Works*, ed. Lady Trevelyan (London, 1875), V, 122–23.

33. *Ibid.*, pp. 131, 144.

34. Quoted by J. H. Plumb, *The Making of an Historian* (*Collected Essays*, vol. I; Athens, Ga., 1988), p. 183.

35. Terry Eagleton, *Literary Theory: An Introduction* (Minneapolis, 1983), p. 145. Another Marxist, Frederic Jameson, complains that Foucault paralyzes "the impulses of negation and revolt" (quoted by David Couzens Hoy, ed., *Foucault: A Critical Reader* [Oxford, 1986], p. 11).

36. Jürgen Habermas, "Modernity Versus Postmodernity," *New German Critique*, Winter 1981, p. 13. Some sources have Ha-

bermas identifying these postmodernists as "Neoconservatives" (e.g., David Couzens Hoy, "Jacques Derrida," in *The Return of Grand Theory in the Human Sciences*, ed. Quentin Skinner [Cambridge, Eng., 1985], p. 61; Lawrence D. Kritzman, ed., Michel Foucault, *Politics, Philosophy, Culture: Interviews and Other Writings 1977–1984* [New York, 1988], p. xi). But he explicitly (and in italics) calls them "Young Conservatives" in contrast to the "Neoconservatives" who accept some of the agenda of modernity— most notably, science and capitalist growth. See also Habermas, "Taking Aim at the Heart of the Present," in *Foucault: A Critical Reader*, pp. 103–8; and the comments on this essay by Hubert L. Dreyfus and Paul Rabinow, "What Is Maturity? Habermas and Foucault on 'What Is Enlightenment?,' " in *Foucault: A Critical Reader*, pp. 109–21.

37. Michael Walzer, "The Politics of Michel Foucault," in *Foucault: A Critical Reader*, pp. 55, 67.

38. Mark Poster, *Foucault, Marxism and History: Mode of Production Versus Mode of Information* (Cambridge, Eng., 1984), p. 40.

39. Keith Gandal, "Michel Foucault: Intellectual Work and Politics," *Telos*, Spring 1986, p. 122. See also Rebecca Comay, "Excavating the Repressive Hypothesis," in the same issue of *Telos*; Derek D. Nikolinakos, "Foucault's Ethical Quandary," *Telos*, Spring 1990; Russell A. Berman, "Troping to Pretoria: The Rise and Fall of Deconstruction," *Telos*, Fall 1990.

40. Peter N. Stearns, "Social History Update: Encountering Postmodernism," *Journal of Social History*, 1990, p. 449. For a more extended discussion of the politics of postmodernism, see Peter Shaw, "The Politics of Deconstruction," in *The War Against the Intellect: Episodes in the Decline of Discourse* (Iowa City, 1989); Catherine Zuckert, "The Politics of Derridean Deconstruction," *Polity*, Spring 1991; Jonathan Arar, ed., *Postmodernism and Politics* (Minneapolis, 1986).

41. Eagleton, p. 148. (Italics in the original.)

42. Foucault's last essay, published posthumously, is a labored attempt to reinterpret Kant's "What Is Enlightenment?" so that his own philosophy might appear to be less irreconcilably opposed to the Enlightenment. But the essay does justice neither

to Kant nor to himself (*The Foucault Reader*, ed. Paul Rabinow [New York, 1984], pp. 32–50).

43. Foucault, *Power/Knowledge*, ed. C. Gordon (New York, 1980), p. 131.

44. Derrida, "Living On," in Harold Bloom *et al.*, eds., *Deconstruction and Criticism* (New York, 1990 [1st ed., 1979]), pp. 104–5.

45. White, *The Content of the Form* (Baltimore, 1987), p. 101.

46. *Ibid.*, pp. 60–61.

47. *Ibid.*, pp. 63, 72, 81, 227 (n. 12).

48. Joan Wallach Scott, *Gender and the Politics of History* (New York, 1988), p. 4.

49. Novick, p. 496.

50. Joan B. Landes, *Women and the Public Sphere in the Age of the French Revolution* (Ithaca, N.Y., 1988), pp. 1–2; Scott, pp. 3, 6; Bonnie S. Anderson and Judith P. Zinsser, *A History of Their Own: Women in Europe from Prehistory to the Present* (New York, 1988), p. xviii. See also Philippa Levine, "When Method Matters: Women Historians, Feminist Historians," *Journal of British Studies*, October 1991. Peter Novick claims that by the late 1970s the idea that history could legitimately be written from a feminist perspective "was no longer being argued; it was a settled question, beyond argument" (p. 496).

51. Irene Diamond and Lee Quinby, *Feminism and Foucault: Reflections on Resistance* (Boston, 1988), pp. xv–xvi.

52. James Miller, *The Passion of Michel Foucault* (New York, 1993), p. 389.

53. Ellen Somekawa and Elizabeth A. Smith, "Theorizing the Writing of History or, 'I Can't Think Why It Should Be So Dull, for a Great Deal of It Must Be Invention,' " *Journal of Social History*, 1988, pp. 154–60. (The title of this essay is taken from a remark by a character in Jane Austen's *Northanger Abbey*. Edward Carr used it as the epigraph of *What Is History?* [London, 1961].)

54. For recent statements by "new" as well as traditional historians deploring the "Balkanization" of history, see Gertrude Himmelfarb, "Some Reflections on the New History," *American Historical Review*, 1989, pp. 663–64. The recent proposals for a multicultural curriculum in the schools have stimulated the same

fears. See, for example, Arthur M. Schlesinger, Jr., *The Disuniting of America* (New York, 1992).

55. White, *Tropics of Discourse*, p. 50.

56. Lionel Gossman, *Between History and Literature* (Cambridge, Mass., 1990), p. 289.

57. Lionel Gossman, for example, says that he once welcomed postmodernist history as a "salutary release from the smug certainties of historical positivism," but has come to believe that it promotes a "facile and irresponsible relativism" (Gossman, p. 303). See also Joyce Appleby, "One Good Turn Deserves Another: Moving Beyond the Linguistic: A Response to David Harlan," *American Historical Review*, 1989, pp. 1326–32.

Lawrence Stone exaggerates the movement away from postmodernism when he asserts, first, that "it seems as if at least some of the leaders of the 'linguistic turn' are backing away from this radical elimination of the reality principle" ("History and Post-Modernism," *Past and Present*, May 1992, pp. 192–93). There is a large gap between "at least some" to "nearly everyone." One recalls Stone's earlier prediction of a "revival of narrative," based on such works as Le Roy Ladurie's *Montaillou*, Eric Hobsbawm's *Primitive Rebels*, and E. P. Thompson's *Whigs and Hunters*—none of which is anything like traditional narrative history. That prediction was shortly belied by the postmodernist "linguistic turn," which is even more antithetical to narrative history than the earlier mode of social history.

58. Eagleton, p. 150. For different views of the relationship of postmodernism to the new historicism, see "Patrolling the Borders: Feminist Historiography and the New Historicism," *Radical History Review*, January 1989; *The New Historicism*, ed. H. Aram Veeser (New York, 1989); Brook Thomas, *The New Historicism and Other Old-fashioned Topics* (Princeton, 1991); Frederic Jameson, *Postmodernism: Or, the Cultural Logic of Late Capitalism* (Durham, N.C., 1993).

59. Howard Felperin, *Beyond Deconstruction: The Uses and Abuses of Literary Theory* (Oxford, 1985), p. 72.

60. Eagleton, "Awakening from Modernity," *Times Literary Supplement*, February 20, 1987, p. 194.

61. Derrida, "Cogito and the History of Madness," in *Writing and Difference* (Chicago, 1978), p. 57.

62. Miller, p. 121 (quoting Foucault, *Histoire de la folie à l'âge classique* [Paris, 1972], p. 603).

63. John R. Searle, "The Word Turned Upside Down," *New York Review of Books*, October 27, 1983, p. 77.

64. Higham, p. 103.

65. Derrida, "The Ends of Man," in *Margins of Philosophy* (Chicago, 1982), p. 116.

66. Foucault, *The Order of Things: An Archaeology of the Human Sciences* (New York, 1973 [1st French ed., 1966]), pp. 342–43. White's chapter on Foucault is entitled "Foucault's Discourse: The Historiography of Anti-Humanism" (*Content of the Form*, pp. 104ff.).

67. White, "The Burden of History," p. 133 (*Tropics of Discourse*, p. 49). For critiques of this essay, see Arnaldo Momigliano, "The Rhetoric of History and the History of Rhetoric: On Hayden White's Tropes," *Comparative Criticism: A Yearbook*, 1981, pp. 259–68; G. R. Elton, *Return to Essentials: Some Reflections on the Present State of Historical Study* (Cambridge, Eng., 1991), pp. 27–49.

Index

Gertrude Himmelfarb is Professor Emeritus of History at the Graduate School of the City University of New York. She is a fellow of the British Academy, the Royal Historical Society, the American Philosophical Society, and the American Academy of Arts and Sciences. Her previous books include *Lord Acton: A Study in Conscience and Politics*; *Darwin and the Darwinian Revolution*; *On Liberty and Liberalism: The Case of John Stuart Mill*; *Victorian Minds*; *The Idea of Poverty: England in the Early Industrial Age*; *Marriage and Morals Among the Victorians*; *The New History and the Old*; and *Poverty and Compassion: The Moral Imagination of the Late Victorians*. Miss Himmelfarb has also edited works by Acton, Malthus, and Mill. In 1991 she gave the Jefferson Lecture in the Humanities, under the auspices of the National Endowment for the Humanities.

A NOTE ON THE TYPE

This book was set in a version of Monotype Baskerville, the antecedent of which was a typeface designed by John Baskerville (1706–1775). Baskerville, a writing master in Birmingham, England, began experimenting in about 1750 with type design and punch cutting. His first book, published in 1757 and set throughout in his new types, was a Virgil in royal quarto. It was followed by other famous editions from his press. Baskerville's types, which are distinctive and elegant in design, were a forerunner of what we know today as the "modern" group of typefaces.

Composed by Crane Typesetting Service, Inc.
West Barnstable, Massachusetts
Printed and bound by The Haddon Craftsmen,
Scranton, Pennsylvania
Designed by Brooke Zimmer